Differentiation That Really Works

Grades 6–12

Science

T0321590

Strategies From Real Teachers for Real Classrooms

Differentiation That Really Works

Grades 6–12

Works

Science

Cheryll M. Adams, Ph.D.,
and Rebecca L. Pierce, Ph.D.

PRUFROCK PRESS INC.
WACO, TEXAS

Dedication

This book is dedicated to the many teachers and students with whom we have worked in appreciation for what we have learned from them. We also dedicate this book to our families and friends for their love and support.

Prufrock Press Inc.
P.O. Box 8813
Waco, TX 76714-8813
Phone: (800) 998-2208
Fax: (800) 240-0333
http://www.prufrock.com

CONTENTS

ACKNOWLEDGEMENTS

Although there are many who write in the area of differentiation, the thoughts of Carol Tomlinson have been a tremendous influence on our work and practice. We share her passion for supporting teachers as they design learning environments that meet the needs of diverse learners. She has inspired us to seek out teachers who are practicing professionals and have embraced differentiation. The teachers we selected have or are working toward their license in gifted education. It was our privilege to work with them and we appreciate their willingness to share their work. We gratefully acknowledge the following teachers whose contributions are found in this book:

Jamilyn Bertsch

Tamra Cargile

Deborah Gaff

James Gasaway

Erin Goney

Heather Hall

Vickie Linehan

Cynthia McKee

Abby Meyer

Erin Nolan-Higgins

Deborah Price

David Schuth

Allison Shakinis

Dawn Slein

Deb Smith

Kim Zahrt

CHAPTER 1

INTRODUCTION

Why We Wrote This Book

Many years ago, we were classroom teachers ourselves, and we spent time working with students, trying to understand their needs. We read some of the early work of A. Harry Passow and Sandy Kaplan coming out of the National/State Leadership Training Institute of the 1970s, and thus began our journey toward learning how to differentiate instruction to meet the needs of all of the learners in our classroom. We both found early on in our teaching careers that giving all students the same assignment resulted in some students doing well while others were bored or frustrated. Thus, we learned how to differentiate as a means of surviving and allowing students to thrive. We learned that "more" and "faster" were not better for our gifted students, but that we needed qualitatively different work that centered on broad-based themes, issues, and problems. We learned that, in order to achieve, all of our students required choice and challenge. Now that we have left the precollege classroom and teach at the university level, we still have to differentiate to meet the needs of our undergraduate and graduate students.

Currently, we work together at the Center for Gifted Studies and Talent Development on a number of projects related to differentiated instruction and meeting the needs of learners in the classroom. The center is located in Burris Laboratory School on the campus of Ball State University. The proximity of the center to the Laboratory School provides us the opportunity to work with teachers and students on a regular basis so that we do not lose the important connection to what is actually happening in classrooms today. Working in the Laboratory School and in other schools throughout the United States, we have been able to use our practitioners' and researchers' lens to identify strategies that work well in the classroom.

The strategies that we have chosen to include in this book had to meet several criteria: (1) be easy to implement, (2) be easy to modify, (3) encourage student engagement, (4) have inherent opportunities for differentiation, and (4) be appropriate for multiple grade levels. The strategies we've selected are not an exhaustive list of differentiation strategies, but they are the ones that we see most often being used by real teachers who differentiate well. Although there is little empirical evidence to support the use of these strategies, the practice-based evidence is widespread (Coil, 2007; Gregory & Chapman, 2002; Kingore, 2004; Tomlinson, 2003; Winebrenner, 1992). We think these strategies are vital for teachers to have in their bag of tricks if they want to provide choice and challenge for all learners in their classroom. However, quality differentiating requires more than just a simple bag of tricks.

Working with teachers for more than 14 years nationally and internationally, we found some who were differentiating to a high degree and some who were just beginning to differentiate. We found some who did it well and some who struggled. Comparing and contrasting those teachers who differentiated well from their colleagues who struggled allowed us to zero in on classroom components that seemed to make the difference. What we found is that many teachers were using strategies to differentiate instruction but lacked the management to facilitate multiple groups working on different activities. Others had interesting lessons and activities but when some students finished early, chaos was present. Some teachers differentiated a lesson by providing several paths to reach the same goal, but all students were required to complete the same assessment. Those teachers who had the most successful classrooms not only used differentiated learning strategies but also made use of anchoring activities, classroom management, and differentiated assessment. Realizing that these four components are necessary led to the development of our model, Creating an Integrated Response for Challenging Learners Equitably: A Model by Adams and Pierce (CIRCLE MAP; Adams & Pierce, 2006). We have realized that when teachers have all four components clearly articulated and they implement them, the stage is set for successful differentiation.

We learned something else with our teachers: No matter the level of experience or the effectiveness of differentiation, everyone's issue was time. We have had the privilege to come in contact with teachers who differentiate in their classrooms on a daily basis. These classrooms are "pockets of excellence," where teachers embrace the differentiation mindset and look at everything they do through the differentiation lens. We felt other teachers could gain some time by using lessons that practicing professionals have already created and tested in their own classrooms. The lessons in this book focus on middle and high school science and can be used as written or modified to meet the needs of your own science classroom. We have provided templates that can be used to develop your own materials using the strategies included here.

How Is This Book Different From Every Other Book on Differentiated Strategies?

This book is different because real teachers designed the lessons. Practicing professionals (everyday classroom teachers in the trenches) tested them in their own heterogeneous classrooms. These professionals differentiate on a regular basis. We have included comments for each lesson from the teacher who developed it, describing how to use the strategy and how his or her students responded to the activity. In addition, on many lessons, we have included comments from other teachers who reacted to it.

How to Use This Book

The following steps should be kept in mind as you make your way through the book:
1. Choose the strategy you want to implement.
2. Look at the sample lessons.
3. Don't be afraid to modify a lesson to fit your grade level and the needs of your own students.
4. Use the template to design your own lesson.
5. Use it in your classroom and enjoy!

CIRCLE MAP Model

What Is Differentiation?

Although its early focus denoted modifying curricula to meet the needs of the gifted and talented (Passow, 1982; Ward, 1980), differentiation has since taken center stage as a means of meeting the needs of academically diverse students in the heterogeneous classroom through modifying the curriculum and learning experiences of these students (Tomlinson, 1999, 2001, 2003). Differentiation is not a collection of strategies; it is not simply offering students choices; it is not group work. Although these options may be found in a differentiated classroom, differentiation involves finding multiple ways to structure learning so that each student has an opportunity to work at a moderately challenging level. It is an organized, yet flexible, way of proactively adjusting teaching and learning to meet students where they are, while helping all students achieve maximum growth as learners (Tomlinson, 1999). Put succinctly, differentiation is a mindset, a lens to use in examining every aspect of the classroom. Instruction may be differentiated in content, process, product, learning environment, and affect according to the students' readiness, interest, or learning profiles. For example, all of the students may be studying force and motion (content), but the laboratory experiments in which they participate may be at varying levels of complexity to accommodate their academic readiness for a particular task (process).

Successful differentiation will occur in the classroom when a number of essential elements also are addressed. These essential elements include specific classroom management techniques that address the special needs of a differentiated classroom through flexible use of time, space, and student groups; planned use of anchoring activities; a variety of differentiated instructional strategies; and differentiated assessment (Adams & Pierce, 2006).

The Model

Having worked with preservice and in-service teachers over the last decade to help implement differentiated instructional strategies in their classrooms, we have noticed several commonalities among teachers who are successful. As a result of this research, we developed the CIRCLE MAP model. The CIRCLE MAP, shown in Figure 1, is appropriate for any grade level and content area. It weaves together four elements—classroom management techniques, anchoring activities, differentiated instructional strategies, and differentiated assessment—that we found as the commonalities among teachers who differentiated successfully. Having observed teachers across the country and internationally, we found these elements consistently in classrooms that addressed the needs of all children. For a complete discussion of the model, see Adams and Pierce (2006).

Our purpose in writing this book is to introduce you to a variety of strategies that may be used to assist you in differentiating curriculum and instruction in your own classroom. We make the assumption that you have a good working knowledge of the differentiation mindset. If you don't, we would encourage you to read Carol Tomlinson's (1999, 2001, 2003) work for a complete discussion of the topic.

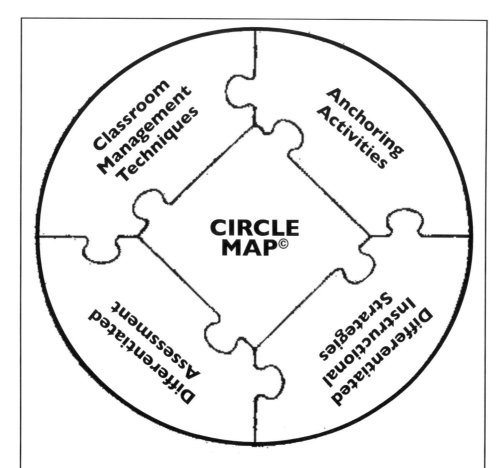

Figure 1. Creating an Integrated Response for Challenging Learners Equitably: A Model by Adams and Pierce©.

CHAPTER 2

EXIT CARDS

Overview

An exit card is a tool used by teachers to gather data about student learning. Generally, exit cards are used to gather formative data that a teacher can then use to plan the next step. The exit card is provided to students at the end of a lesson and the teacher collects the cards as students either exit the classroom or exit one activity before going on to the next in the same classroom. Exit cards also may be known by other names, such as ticket to leave or door pass. Exit cards generally only have a few questions for students to answer. Sometimes the card may ask students to respond to an overall idea that was discussed in class; at other times students may have two or three math problems to work on that are similar to problems demonstrated in class.

How and When to Use Exit Cards

Exit cards are used at the end of a class, an activity, or a lesson. The teacher collects the completed exit cards and sorts the cards into piles based on the students' responses. There may be a group of students who clearly understand the ideas presented in the lesson and another group of students who clearly have gaps in their knowledge. There may be other students who fall between the two groups. The information from the exit cards allows the teacher to plan the next steps of instruction to address the different learning needs of the students.

Directions for Making Exit Cards

Exit cards are simple to design. For example, an exit card can be a piece of paper that the student uses to write down answers to a set of questions dictated by the teacher. Students may use their own paper or the teacher may hand out paper from the classroom recycle box. Index cards and Post-It® Notes also are simple and easy to use as exit cards, although somewhat more expensive. Some teachers may wish to customize their exit cards for a specific lesson or activity.

How This Strategy Fits in the CIRCLE MAP

Exit cards are an important data-gathering tool for formative assessment in the differentiated classroom. As such, they are essential to the "differentiated assessment" component of the CIRCLE MAP.

Examples

The examples we have chosen include exit cards that can be readily adapted to many topics. These cards were created by real teachers who used them in their own classrooms. When possible, we have included the comments from the teachers and their colleagues with the intention that the comments may provide additional insight to using the exit card for another topic.

For example, Janet McCorkle is a middle school science teacher who has decided to implement exit cards in her class this year. She creates a card to help her determine who understands the sequence of steps in mitosis. She designs a card that includes descriptions of each step. Putting these steps in order will establish whether or not students understand the steps in this process. As she collects the cards, Janet can easily determine who has complete, partial, or little understanding of the material. This will allow her to determine the entry point for each student in the next lesson.

Template

Title

Directions/Questions

Roller Coasters—A Math and Science Lab

What did you learn?

Plus – What helped you apply skills?

Delta – What could have been better?

What else do you want to know?

Created by Deborah Gaff

Real Teacher Comments

We have been working on energy transformations in science class. In math class, students are reviewing slopes, properties of triangles, and diameter and areas of circles. I worked with the math teacher to incorporate student-built roller coasters into our lessons. From my perspective, this was a great lesson: I heard science and math vocabulary being used as students tried to create the most thrilling roller coaster ride for their marbles. I am also working on the students' continued engagement in learning. This exit card was designed to let students know that I valued how they thought the lesson went, what they learned, what they liked, and what they still needed to know.

Here are some sample answers to the question of what students learned: "Slope controls speed"; "How to work with people we do not usually work with" (I assigned groups); "More gravitational energy = more kinetic energy"; "Gravity has much to do with roller coasters"; "More gravitational energy = bigger loop"; and "Designing coasters takes talent and practice."

In response to the question of what helped them apply skills, students responded with the following: "Working with others"; "The instructions were not specific"; "We had plenty of time to have other ideas to make a better coaster" (it was an extended period); "Experimenting with different mass"; and "Using our imaginations."

Finally, in response to the question of what else students wanted to know, they said: "Can we have more materials?"; "Challenge the other class to build the longest coaster with the most loops"; "We should have a Saturday to build coasters and then have our parents come in and see them"; "More space"; and "One person in our group did not help."

—Deborah Gaff (Teacher)

Exit Card

We have been discussing that technology involves trade-offs. Briefly discuss two benefits and two drawbacks of the invention of the cell phone.

_____

_____

_____

_____

_____

_____

_____

_____

_____

_____

_____

_____

_____

_____

_____

Created by James Gasaway

Real Teacher Comments

I found this exit card interesting. The exit card would provide a specific analysis of how well students grasped a concept and how I should proceed the next day. We do everything we can to cut paper and copying costs for the school, so I made my exit card a slide to display to the class. The students responded on the back of a scratch paper.

I made the prompt very specific because we had already done some examples as part of a class discussion, and I didn't want students just writing ideas that we had already generated. I was pleased that most students were able to differentiate between benefits and drawbacks (my prompt) and could generate reasonable possibilities based on their own experiences. The students enjoyed coming up with examples, and this technique allowed everyone to participate.

—James Gasaway (Teacher)

I like the way you pulled the cell phone in as an integral part of technology. Many forget to include it when dealing with technology in school. Thanks for the idea!

—Loretta (Colleague)

Anatomy and Physiology
Lymphatic System Exit Card

Your territory is being invaded! You need to keep the enemy at bay.
Assume the role of the general in the army of the body's defenses. Give orders to
your two groups of defenders, nonspecific defense and specific defense. Tell them
what to attack, how to attack, and when to attack.

◊ Nonspecific defense system: _____

_____

_____

_____

_____

_____

_____

◊ Specific defense system: _____

_____

_____

_____

_____

_____

_____

_____

Do not write here—teacher use only.   3   2   1

Created by Heather Hall

Real Teacher Comments

Attached is the exit card that I created to be used in my Anatomy and Physiology class. This would be used as we began our study of the lymphatic system. I would use the bottom right-hand area to mark the level of understanding of a particular student. Here is what those numbers mean to me:

3. You've got it—you're ready to move on.
2. You're getting there.
1. You need some more help.

—Heather Hall (Teacher)

I like your analogy. I could use this when we talk about first- and second-line defenses of the body. Our book even uses a graphic of a knight in armor to illustrate this concept.

—Sharon (Colleague)

That is very creative. Practical and humorous!

—Tina (Colleague)

Thanks! I think the students seem to better understand body systems when I can make a comparison to something that they know already, such as an army. They seem to enjoy the use of humor whenever possible—as do I!

—Heather (Teacher)

OH, SUGAR SUGAR

Imagine you are heading home after practice, and you still have to eat before homework and bedtime. Your parents offer to take you to a fast food restaurant to save time. Identify three ways you could reduce your sugars and make healthy food choices at a not-so-healthy food spot.

1._____

_____

2._____

_____

3._____

_____

List at least one pro and at least one con to sugar consumption.

PRO	CON

Created by Erin Nolan-Higgins

Real Teacher Comments

I am working on a health and wellness unit, guiding students to make positive eating/lifestyle choices. For this lesson, we talked about the effects of sugar in our diet. They were instructed to select a meal of interest from a variety of fast food choices. The choices included nutritional information, but the nutritional facts were not factored into their initial choices. Upon selecting their meals, including drinks, students were to locate the sugar contents and record the amount of sugar in grams contained in the meals they had selected. Then they converted the sugar from grams to teaspoons. Finally, they simulated the amount of sugar consumed in teaspoons by measuring out the correct amount of sugar and placing it into a plastic cup.

As we discussed each step along the way, actually seeing how much sugar they consumed in one meal was an eye-opener for them! This led to us talking about how to make healthier choices in a not-so-healthy environment. The exit card was a great way to reflect on what students had learned, because each student could make a personal connection to, and therefore a more informed decision about, alternative food choices and/or portion sizes.

—Erin Nolan-Higgins (Teacher)

I really like your exit card, especially because I am a big advocate for health and wellness. I like that it puts students in a real-life situation. It allows you to see whether they gained the necessary knowledge and understanding and gets them to start thinking about how to apply that knowledge to their own lives. Hopefully, next time they go to a not-so-healthy food place, they will be thinking about your lesson.

—Daniel (Colleague)

Great application to the real world! Sometimes our students question why we have to learn certain things, and the fast food scenario is the real world for them. The more we relate our lessons to the lives of our students, I believe, the better the understanding.

—Sharon (Colleague)

What a benefit for the kids to sit down and think of how to limit their sugars at a yummy fast food place! Very cool topic!

—Kimberly (Colleague)

Circulation Lab Exit Card

List two things you learned about circulation in animals.

Complete the following sentence: After doing this lab, I have a greater understanding of . . .

Complete the following sentence: After doing this lab, I would like to find out more about . . . .

Created by Deborah Price

Real Teacher Comments

I gave this exit card to my AP Biology class today after they did a lab on circulation and how blood pressure and heart rate are affected by body position, activity level, fitness, and temperature. The student responses demonstrated that they had learned the main objectives in the lab. A few cards had some misunderstandings, and I can clear those up next class period. The prompt that asked students what they would like to learn more about was very interesting. They came up with some ideas that could be used to extend the lab further. Others came up with topics that they may want to choose for their final semester projects. What I liked best was the instant feedback and the new ideas that came from the students themselves. I know I will be using exit cards more often in all my classes.

—Deborah Price (Teacher)

I usually see exit cards for reading and sometimes math skills. It was very nice to get an idea of how to use exit cards with science. I also like the way you went from recall to higher level thinking questions. I sometimes forget that I can find out more than simply whether a student recalls a name, setting, and so on. I will have to remember to do some more exit cards with these types of prompts and different subject areas.

—Amy (Colleague)

I'm glad you found the exit cards as useful and informative as I did! It is such an easy and simple strategy, but one that I haven't taken the time to use in the past. I too will be using them more often!

—Kerri (Colleague)

I really like the idea of using the exit card to follow a lab. I know that we as teachers are often so busy with the mechanics of the lab—gathering supplies, making sure that stations are cleaned and reset for the next group, answering procedural questions, and so on—that we never get much time to process the lab as a group until the next class meeting, if ever. The exit card is an excellent way to make sure that each individual is accountable for demonstrating his or her processing of the content of the lab. Often, labs are done (and processed) by one person in the group, and everyone else rides on that person's coattails. I would say that this type of postlab exit card would be most effective if it were given out after the lab groups had already disbanded, if possible, so that the more dominant members of the group were not available for the weaker group members once again to rely on for gathering significance from the lab.

—Deena (Colleague)

Exit Card: Subatomic Particles

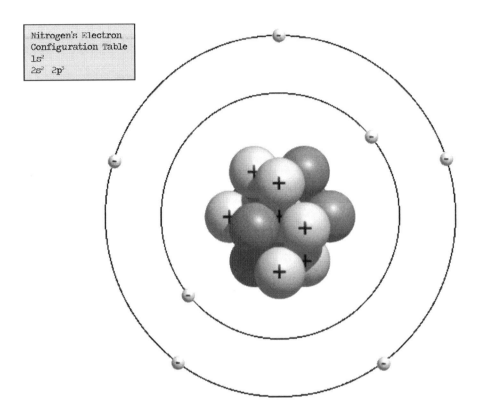

Nitrogen's Electron
Configuration Table
$1s^2$
$2s^2$ $2p^3$

On your exit card, explain the differences among protons,
neutrons, and electrons. You may wish to use ions and
isotopes as part of your explanation.

Created by David Schuth

Real Teacher Comments

I wanted to be sure that students could distinguish between protons, neutrons, and electrons. I also wanted to be sure that they knew how ions and isotopes were related to these particles. From my exit card, I was able to determine the knowledge level of all of my students. This way, I could design appropriate reteaching or extension activities for the next class meeting.

—David Schuth (Teacher)

I like your exit card. My students often get protons and neutrons confused. By using this card, I could easily see which students had learned the concept and which students did not.

—Tina (Colleague)

Exit Card

1. List the steps of DNA replication. _____

    _____

    _____

    _____

    _____

    _____

2. Use two colored pencils to sketch the results of DNA replication.

3. Identify and state the function of **two** enzymes involved in DNA replication.

    _____

    _____

    _____

    _____

4. What is one question you have about how DNA replicates? _____

    _____

    _____

    _____

    _____

Created by Dawn Slein

Real Teacher Comments

Exit cards are new to me. They are similar to a certain type of journal entry that I have used for many years. All of my students have spiral notebooks that stay in my classroom. We use these journals for openers, notes, minilabs, diagrams, and writings on discussion topics.

This card was used after an introduction to DNA replication in general biology. Students watched a couple of animations multiple times. We discussed what was happening in each animation, pausing to be able to identify the steps and key elements to DNA replication. Then we compared textbook diagrams and each student wrote and sketched what he or she knew about the DNA replication. After private sketching, the students were allowed to discuss and compare with another student in the room, adding to or modifying their diagrams. Groups of students listed the elements of a superior diagram on small white boards. An agreed-upon class list of needed elements was established and written on the board. A question-and-answer session took place, followed by watching the animations one more time.

The next day, one animation was used to answer all of the questions the class had on replication. This was a great way to review the previous day's material, and the discussion was directed into the next topic.

My students are used to the discussion/ sketch/discussion format. Usually I will have students leave their journals open so that I can cruise around the room and check their work. But this exit card was a great way to see just how much information students could pick up in one class period. The instant feedback was great. I could evaluate how much more time to spend on replication, as well as what specific steps of the process needed more review.

—Dawn Slein (Teacher)

I think what I like best about the exit card is the instant feedback that can help you plan for the next day.

—Deborah (Colleague)

I like that the last question on the ticket is asking them to write a question. That makes them really think about their understanding of DNA, and it also helps you measure their level of thought. This could lead to some awesome critical thinking opportunities and push students to synthesize.

—Amelia (Colleague)

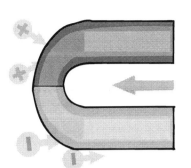 

Physics Exit Card

In the space below, solve the problem that is on the board. First copy the problem in the space below, and then begin solving it. Use the back of this sheet if necessary, but leave enough space on the back for your learning comment(s).

Created by Kim Zahrt

Real Teacher Comments

I made this exit card for my AP Physics students. I made the cards larger than the usual 3" x 5" index cards, because the students will need more room to answer the questions. They will be allowed 15–20 minutes because of the complexity of the problems they solve.

I plan to score the exit card as follows:

4 – The answer is correct, and instructions were followed.

3 – The answer is almost correct, but following instructions was an issue.

2 – Some parts of the answer are correct, but the student didn't follow instructions.

1 – None of the answer is correct, and the student had difficulty following instructions.

—Kim Zahrt (Teacher)

Your scoring guide really helped me see how you used the cards. I like the scoring/grouping category descriptions. I think I could also use something similar when we are calculating speed, velocity, and so on. There always seem to be a few who are unable to get the concept, and this seems to be a good way to decide grouping for reteaching.

—Tamara (Colleague)

After looking at your plan, it struck me that in the secondary setting, it seems that if a teacher were to do exit cards on a regular basis, it would be something done more on a weekly basis, as opposed to daily. The concepts are usually more difficult, and to get even a quick insight into students' comprehension and feedback requires more time.

—Laura (Colleague)

I agree with your thoughts about time limitations. A lengthy reply from every student requires more teacher time. In order to check the higher level thinking skills of these high-ability students, the questions do require more student thinking time and teacher sorting time. I hadn't thought of the feedback aspect until you brought it up.

—Jeri (Colleague)

CHAPTER 3

CHOICE BOARDS

Overview

A choice board, sometimes called a Tic-Tac-Toe board, is a tool to provide students with choice and challenge. It has nine squares in a three by three array. Directions are placed in each square. Students choose three squares to complete to make a winning tic-tac-toe: three in a row, three in a column, or three diagonally. The directions may be for a product or for extended practice. Choices can provide enrichment, acceleration, or additional practice, depending on how the choice board is designed. Generally, students are producing three products, which would provide formative or summative data for the teacher.

How and When to Use Choice Boards

Choice boards can be used at the beginning or end of a unit or anywhere in between. The length of time students have to complete their three choices varies with the teacher's purpose. Some choice boards are designed to be completed in a week (e.g., one that deals with weekly spelling words). Other times, a choice board may last for longer periods of time, depending on the complexity of the choices or the length of time the teacher chooses for activities to be completed. Choice boards may be tiered to accommodate varying learning needs when a wider range of choices and challenge is needed. The completed activities from the choice board can be used by the teacher to plan the next steps of instruction, to assess students' progress or level of understanding, or as a means of assigning grades.

Directions for Making Choice Boards

Choice boards are simple to design using the template provided here. The table function in a word processing program is another easy way to create choice boards. Each cell contains directions for or a description of an activity to be completed. Once the activities are appropriately sequenced to allow for variety no matter how the student chooses to make tic-tac-toe, the choice board can then be printed and copied. We have found that putting the activities on Post-It® Notes allows for experimentation with multiple arrangements until the "best" placement is found. Then we use a word processing program to produce the final form of the choice board for students. Choose the way that works best with your particular style of creating classroom materials. Keep in mind that some activities will require rubrics while others may be self-checking and students will need to know where to find answer keys.

How This Strategy Fits in the CIRCLE MAP

Choice boards fit in the "differentiated instructional strategies" component of the CIRCLE MAP. They provide a simple yet lively means to vary the process or product in a differentiated classroom.

Examples

The examples we have chosen to include here address specific topics. These choice boards were created by real teachers who used them in their own classrooms. When possible, we have included the comments from the teachers and their colleagues with the intention that the comments may provide additional insight to creating your own choice board. We have tried to include a wide variety of topics to give you a number of ideas for making your own.

For example, in Carter Smith's honors eighth-grade Earth science class, students are busily working on a choice board he has designed as part of his unit on plate tectonics. In each of the nine blocks, he has placed an interesting activity to reinforce or enrich the concepts he has chosen. Carter has been careful to include activities that will appeal to various strengths and learning profiles. He has developed some activities that encourage written responses and some that are more analytic. Some activities require research, and some rely on reinforcing facts. By providing activities at a variety of readiness levels, as well as addressing different learning profiles, he has ensured that his students will find challenging and meaningful activities to complete.

Template
Title of Choice Board

Directions: Please select three assignments to complete for a winning tic-tac-toe (3 in the same row, 3 in the same column, or 3 diagonally).

Newton's Choices

Directions: Select one activity in each column so that your chosen activities complete a tic-tac-toe to demonstrate your understanding of forces.

For activities 3, 6, and 9, you may work with the lab partner of your choice.

Activities are due: _____

Complete a Frayer Model Map for the word "force." **1**	Create a model of a roller coaster and label where laws of force and motion apply. You must include a written explanation. **2**	Create a poster illustrating each of Newton's three laws. Use real-life examples for your illustrations. **3**
Create a PowerPoint vocabulary quiz using vocabulary pertaining to force. **4**	Calculate the answers to the questions found at this site: http://schools.mukilteo. wednet.edu/staff/davisad/8s ci/53CALCULATINGFO RCEWORKSHEET.pdf **5**	Create a video briefly demonstrating each of Newton's three laws. **6**
Create a vocabulary study guide with illustrations. The study guide can be made of note cards or can be a folded study guide. **7**	In California's Death Valley, there is a dry lakebed known as Racetrack, Playa, where rocks mysteriously move. Investigate this phenomenon and explain what is happening. **8**	Create a primer introducing Newton's three laws to seventh graders. **9**

Created by Deborah Gaff

Real Teacher Comments

We are finishing a chapter about Newton's three laws of motion. I am making sure students know the vocabulary, can apply the knowledge, and can explain the knowledge to others. I have included some "safe" choices, as I have students for whom the material is brand new and others for whom it is review. The students enjoyed the choices, and I'm happy to say that every block was chosen by at least one student.

—Deborah Gaff (Teacher)

Tic-Tac-Toe Board
Integrated Chemistry/Physics

D. Hodgkin	J. Kepler	N. Bohr
J. Dalton	M. Curie	E. Rutherford
E. Fermi	M. Goeppert-Mayer	R. Yalow

BROCHURE Create a brochure that details the contributions to science of this scientist. Include pictures and text.	**CURRENT ARTICLE** Find an article in the news today that is related to the contributions of this scientist.	**POWERPOINT** Create and present a PowerPoint that details the life and works of the scientist.
POSTER Create a poster display that shows the works of the scientist. This should include pictures and text.	**ROLE-PLAY** Give a presentation to the class in character. You will describe your work from the perspective of the scientist. You should come in costume. Props are optional.	**OBITUARY** Read an obituary to understand the format. Write an obituary for the scientist. Be sure to include the person's background, obstacles in life, education, and so on.
JOB APPLICATION Access a job application. Complete the job application as though you were a particular scientist. You'll have to do some digging to find out information related to things like education, skills, training, and so on.	**SCRAPBOOK** Create a scrapbook that shows the life and times of the scientist.	**MODEL** Create a 3-D model of something that has been discovered or has resulted from the work of the scientist.

Created by Heather Hall

Real Teacher Comments

My tic-tac-toe board is for Integrated Chemistry Physics. For that class, there are several standards related to historical perspectives. There are nine scientists whose contributions to the advancement of science the students learn about. For my tic-tac-toe board, I created an overlay with the names of those scientists on it. The overlay is clear and can be rotated in any direction to allow for a view of the options below. This way, the students have a choice not only in the activity, but also in the scientists they research. I was very excited to try this out in class! I find that sometimes it can be a bit boring to students to cover the historical perspectives required by the state science standards. I really like the spin this puts on that topic!

—Heather Hall (Teacher)

You have great higher level activities, and I like how they get to decide on the person as well as the products. I think the kids will not only enjoy this, but also get a lot out of it.

—Shannon (Colleague)

I like the way you decided to add the overlay. Great thinking!

—Brenda (Colleague)

I think the idea of choosing their scientist and projects will definitely give the students ownership of this project.

—Megan (Colleague)

As a student in what could be a very difficult course, I would find this activity very engaging.

—Tracy (Colleague)

Ecosystems Tic-Tac-Toe Project Board

★ Choose three projects that make a tic-tac-toe.
★ Any of the projects may be done about any of the biomes we have studied:
  ❑ temperate deciduous forest,
  ❑ temperate rainforest,
  ❑ tropical rainforest,
  ❑ tundra,
  ❑ taiga,
  ❑ desert,
  ❑ freshwater ecosystems, or
  ❑ saltwater ecosystems.
★ The children's books and the ABC frieze may be done with a partner (the maximum number of students is two).
★ Class work days with computers will be posted.
★ Project due dates will be posted.
★ You may choose to complete another project for 25 extra credit points.

Write **10 journal entries** from the point of view of a plant or tree that is host to animals and insects in its biome.	Write and illustrate a **children's book** all about a particular biome.	Create a two-sided (six-panel) **travel brochure** in Microsoft Publisher about your biome.
Create an **ABC frieze** using plants, animals, and resources from a specific biome.	Make a **tic-tac-toe poster** using nine pictures and nine facts about a particular biome.	Write **10 journal entries** from the point of view of an animal travelling through a certain biome.
Write a one-page **newsletter** in Microsoft Publisher about your biome.	Create a **multimedia presentation** that could be shown to elementary classrooms about a specific biome.	Write and illustrate a **children's book** about a rock that has witnessed all of the steps of primary succession.

Journal Entries (Plant or Tree)

★ You are a plant or tree that is host to animals and insects in your biome.

★ Be very specific about:

❑ the type of plant or tree you are,

❑ the climate and location of your biome,

❑ how long you have been there and what changes to your environment you have witnessed,

❑ the insects and animals that may use you as food or shelter, and

❑ any interactions you have with humans (are humans a threat to your survival?).

★ Make sure that time passes between journal entries. (You might span an entire year, showing the changes in seasons in your biome through your entries.)

★ Each entry should be minimum 1/2 page typed and should include a picture (from the computer or drawn)—if you use pictures found on the Internet, cite your sources!

★ Make a clever cover for your journal.

ABC Frieze

★ Create an ABC frieze using plants, animals, resources, and so on from a specific biome.

★ This may be done with a partner.

★ A frieze is a series of pictures with captions that can be laminated and hung as a banner.

★ Be very specific about animals, plants, resources, people groups, or other things from your biome.

★ Be creative! An example would be Q for "Quiet place," X for "X-cellent seafood," Y for "You would like it there," and Z for "Zzz . . . shh! Animals sleeping!"

★ Each letter should be on a separate 8 1/2" x 11" sheet of paper.

Newsletter

★ Write a one-page newsletter about your biome.

★ Use any template in Microsoft Publisher and write headlines and articles about your biome.

★ Include animals, plants, climate, landscape, and human influence (both good and bad).

★ Use pictures sparingly—make them count for more than page filler!

★ Cite your picture sources.

Children's Book (Biome)

★ This activity may be done with a partner.

★ Each page should cover a different aspect of your biome.

★ Plants, animals, climate, landscape, human influence (good and bad), interesting facts, and pictures should be covered.

★ Cite your picture sources.

★ Your book should have a minimum of 10 pages plus a clever cover.

Tic-Tac-Toe Poster

★ Divide a poster board into nine equal sections.

★ Use the center section for your title (it's not about you!).

★ In each of the remaining eight sections, have a picture and a fact about your biome.

★ Vary your facts about plants, animals, climate, landscape, human influence (good and bad), and resources.

Multimedia Presentation

★ This can be a PowerPoint, PhotoStory3, or DVD about your biome.

★ Make sure you cover plants, animals, climate, landscape, human influence (good and bad), and resources.

Travel Brochure

★ Create a two-sided (six-panel) travel brochure about your biome. Use any appropriate Microsoft Publisher template.

★ Use pictures sparingly and appropriately.

★ Cite your sources.

★ Sell your biome—why should somebody want to visit?

Journal Entries (Animal)

★ You are an animal travelling through your biome.

★ Be very specific about:

❑ the type of animal you are;

❑ the climate and location of your biome;

❑ how long you have been there and what changes to your environment you have witnessed;

❑ where you are on the food chain (what predators eat you, and what prey do you eat?); and

❑ any interactions you have with humans (are humans a threat to your survival?).

★ Make sure that time passes between journal entries. (You might span an entire year, showing the changes in seasons in your biome through your entries.)

★ Each entry should be minimum 1/2 page typed and should include a picture (from the computer or drawn)—if you use pictures found on the Internet, cite your sources!

★ Make a clever cover for your journal.

Children's Book (Rock)

★ This may be done with a partner.

★ Create the character of a talking rock that has survived and witnessed all of the steps of primary succession.

★ Write and illustrate one page per step of primary succession.

★ Pictures can be drawn, computer generated, taken from the Internet (cite your sources), or a combination.

★ Make a clever cover and a surprising ending!

Created by Vickie Linehan

Real Teacher Comments

I use variations of choice boards all of the time for all of my classes. My students like the ability to "choose their own grades" by choosing their activities. At first I was frustrated by this approach, because it does take work to create the activities. Teaching inner-city kids, I find I need to encourage them to take advantage of challenging opportunities. Last year I created at least one unit with a "Choose Your Own Grade" option each grading period. This year, I'll add another unit for each grading period. Working at this pace allows me to build on past successes and tweak activities that weren't such a big hit. Anyway, my KEY (highest ability) class created this tic-tac-toe board based on their project preferences. They had a really good suggestion—staggered due dates for the projects. I thought it was a good idea, and I was willing to give it a shot. Both of my high-ability classes liked the projects, and they're buzzing about doing it again!

—Vickie Linehan (Teacher)

I often run my class in a similar way. The kids are able to use their personal interests and talents to explore new areas about a topic. They like it, and it is a lot more fun for me as well.

—Quella (Colleague)

I really like the idea of projects, and I can adapt this to my own situation.

—Allison (Colleague)

ROCKS AND MINERALS
Choice Board

Explain the differences among carrot, karat, and carat.	Register yourself at www.scilinks.org. Go to Topic: The Rock Identification Key, SciLinks code HSM0782. Tell me something you found that was new to you.	Make a list of safety equipment needed by a miner.
Develop a new gemstone. How is it made? What minerals are used? What are its special qualities? Where is it found? What color is it? What is the cut of your stone? Design a piece of jewelry for your gemstone.	Create a PowerPoint presentation about Moh's scale of mineral hardness.	Register yourself at www.scilinks.org. Go to Topic: Minerals and Metals, SciLinks code HSM0968. What mineral impressed you the most, and why?
Find information on Black Lung Disease. How has technology minimized its occurrence?	Using a penny, a pencil, and your fingernail, rank the materials in order from softest to hardest. (Use the graphite tip of the pencil.) Why might there be a discrepancy among other students' results?	Explain to a farmer whose farm is along U.S. Route 50 why he or she should use contour plowing or terracing. Be sure to give reasons to convince the farmer to use your advice.

Created by Cynthia McKee

Real Teacher Comments

I created this choice board as a way for my students to review the information we have been studying about rocks and minerals. I find that the website www.scilinks.org has great resource materials for middle and high school students. These activities allow students to work on their own to get a better understanding of the material. By far the most popular choice was the create-your-own-gemstone activity.

—Cynthia McKee (Teacher)

I teach this same topic, and I am going to give your choice board a try when it's time to teach this material. I liked that the variety of choices ranged from simple to complex.

—Quella (Colleague)

Chemistry
States of Matter Choice Board

Choose three activities on the board to make a winning tic-tac-toe. Do the
activities on a separate sheet of paper and attach it to this sheet.

Explain why it takes longer to cook food in water at high altitudes.	Describe how the movement of particles changes with changes in temperature. Be sure to explain both an increase and a decrease in temperature.	Explain the role of atmospheric pressure when you drink through a straw.
Explain how the movement of gas particles creates pressure.	Does surface area of a liquid affect the rate of evaporation? Form a hypothesis and describe a procedure that would test this idea.	Make a model of the crystal structure of calcite.
Give an everyday example of evidence that all particles of matter are in constant motion.	Compare and contrast evaporation and boiling.	Is H_2O at 0 degrees Celsius a solid or a liquid? Justify your response.

Created by Deborah Price

Real Teacher Comments

I used this board to introduce the next chapter in my chemistry class. I took a sampling of topics so the students would be introduced to some of the different ideas from the chapter.

Some positives from this activity were that the students liked having choices and my higher ability kids had a lot of trouble choosing because they found so many of the ideas interesting.

There were also some negatives from the activity. Students wanted to make all of the easy choices—they did not like that I arranged the choices so that there was a mix of easy and more difficult ideas in each tic-tac-toe. Some of the students answered in a very shallow way, but that is no different than if I had assigned textbook questions. Some students tried guessing the answers without using their resources and then expected me to tell them if their guesses were correct.

Overall, I think this was a good way to introduce a new chapter, because the students left the classroom thinking about what we would learn and how it could apply to real situations. Next time, I will indicate in the directions that all items are worth the same number of points, and I would be more specific about the depth of thought I wanted in students' answers.

—Deborah Price (Teacher)

Your choices seem like very meaningful introductory activities. I thought there was a wide variety of options and skill levels.

—Melissa (Colleague)

I like how you made this a one-day activity. I was thinking it had to take a few days. Your introduction to the chapter is a great way to get students talking!

—Dawn (Colleague)

Chemistry Choice Board

Students must pick one activity from each column to make tic-tac-toe.

With a partner, decipher an alien periodic table and predict where all of the elements belong.	Create your own chemistry comic strip about electrons. The strip should be at least three panels long.	Categorize elements based upon their valence in your own periodic table that you create.
Describe the pattern of the atomic sizes of atoms by color coding the trends within a periodic table.	Hypothesize what happens in atoms in order to achieve a valence of 8 and complete a 2-minute journalistic investigation video about those atoms' inner struggles.	Summarize the electron fill order in an atom by creating an energy budget for the first 40 electrons in an atom.
Clarify the reactivity trends in the periodic table by creating a cookbook with recipes for seven metals and seven nonmetals.	Generate a scavenger hunt for your classmates where the answers to the clues are always answered with ionic charges.	Apply your knowledge of ionic charges to create a flipchart showing how ions react with each other.

Created by David Schuth

Real Teacher Comments

I created this choice board to help my students gain a better understanding of basic chemistry related to chemical elements. I wanted students to be able to use higher level critical and creative thinking skills to demonstrate their knowledge. The students enjoyed reviewing the material through the choice board rather than through completing worksheets. I was pleasantly surprised at the quality and depth of knowledge the students demonstrated in their completed products. The students stayed engaged throughout the activities—quite a feat for middle school students!

—David Schuth (Teacher)

Choice Board for

Characteristics of Life

Choose one activity from **each** column to complete a tic-tac-toe.

1. In your own words, describe the six characteristics that all living things share.	2. Complete the minilab *Is It Alive?* at faculty.ivytech.edu/~bsipe/is_it_alive.doc.	3. Use pictures from magazines to create a poster showing three living and three nonliving things. Write a paragraph below each picture explaining the characteristics that identify the thing as living or nonliving.
4. Make up a mnemonic device to help remember the six characteristics of life.	5. What characteristics of living things does a river have? Is a river alive? Explain.	6. Create a drawing of an imaginary life form. All traits of the life form must be based on the main characteristics of life. Provide a short written description of each trait or characteristic that your life form has and explain how each helps the organism survive in the environment in which it lives.
7. Make a chart that lists 10 things that are living and 10 things that are nonliving.	8. Complete a Frayer Model Map for the phrase "living things."	9. Invent a game to help other students learn about six characteristics of life.

I chose activities # _____, # _____, and # _____.

Created by Deb Smith

Real Teacher Comments

I liked the idea of using sticky notes to create the tasks for each square. I think I used up a whole package of them trying to get the activities worded and placed where I wanted them. I was surprised that thinking of the tasks wasn't as hard as I imagined. My problem was succinctly wording each task in the square so it made sense! My hard work paid off, and I now have a choice board for my current topic.

—Deb Smith (Teacher)

CHAPTER 4

CUBING

Overview

Cubing is an instructional strategy that has its roots in writing. The strategy uses a cube; on each face of the cube are directions using an action verb (such as create, compare, and analyze) and under each verb is a prompt providing a description of the task. Students roll the cube and complete the activity from the face of the cube that is turned up. They repeat this procedure until they have completed a total of six different tasks. Cubing can be used at any point in a lesson or unit. Like choice boards, cubing is another way to differentiate instruction. Cubing is a novel way to structure a set of activities and to view a topic from multiple angles.

How and When to Use Cubing

Cubing is a versatile strategy that can easily fit into instructional plans at various points—beginning, middle, or end. A cube may be used to introduce a topic and find out what students already know. It may be used in sense-making activities or as a means to determine what students learned from a particular lesson or unit. Students may have their own individual cube or each group may be given a single cube. Cubes can be tiered to accommodate a variety of student cognitive abilities, skill levels, or knowledge of the topic. Sometimes we have heard questions such as, "Couldn't you just list the activities on a sheet of paper and allow students to do the activities in any order?" Although you certainly could do that, we have found that students respond positively when we use strategies that are "fun." As you will see below in the teacher comments, students who experienced cubing certainly thought it was a fun and exciting way to learn.

Directions for Making Cubes

Cubes are simple to design using the template provided here. Another alternative and a convenient way to acquire sturdy cubes is to purchase small ($3 \times 3 \times 3$) boxes from a packaging company. Printing the activities on mailing labels and affixing them to the box or template is easier than writing directly on either one. If you choose to write directly on the cube, do so while the cube is unfolded using a fine point, felt tip marker. The table function in a word processing program also can be used to create a cube. Form a 3×4 array, keep the first column intact as well as the middle row, and then delete the extraneous six cells. As another option, you may find it convenient to use The Dice Maker at http://www.toolsforeducators.com. No matter how you form the cube, the format for creating the activity on each face is the same: action verb + prompt.

How This Strategy Fits in the CIRCLE MAP

Cubes fit in the "differentiated instructional strategies" component of the CIRCLE Map. They provide a simple yet lively means to vary the content, process, or product in a differentiated classroom.

Examples

The examples we have chosen address specific topics. These cubes were created by real teachers who used them in their own classrooms. When possible, we have included the comments from the teachers and their colleagues with the intention that the comments may provide additional insight to using the cubes. We have tried to include a wide variety of topics to give you a number of ideas for making your own.

For example, Lisa Miller attended a professional development workshop focusing on a variety of strategies that could be used to differentiate instruction. She particularly liked a strategy called "cubing," but she wondered how her AP Chemistry class would respond. She thought they might think using cubes was silly. Her worries proved unnecessary, because when she introduced the activity, the students were excited! During the activity, each group of three students was assigned a cube. An activity that related to their study of the structure of matter was written on each face of the cube. Each activity was challenging and required students to use their critical thinking skills. According to the students, it was a great success, and they would like to have the opportunity to work with cubes again.

Template

HISTORY OF DISEASE

Evaluate the statement that diseases are caused by fluids in the body being out of balance.

Give an example of how technology influences understanding of diseases.

Explain one way that diseases have been viewed in history.

Name something that causes organisms to become ill.

Describe something that happens to an organism when it becomes ill.

Suggest a way to increase disease prevention.

Real Teacher Comments

I decided to use a cube to have groups work to activate prior knowledge and preassess what students knew and believed about our upcoming unit. Students took turns rolling the cubes in groups. They wrote the response to what they rolled and then discussed it with the group. They were not to use the same answer that someone else had already used. I was able to determine that few students knew any information about the history of disease and were focused only on humans when discussing diseases. They very much enjoyed the activity, and it sparked some great debates between the students.

—Tamra Cargile (Teacher)

I love your idea about using the cubes as a preassessment!

—Sonny (Colleague)

I really liked that you used this activity as a preassessment. I realize how beneficial it is to have a preassessment, but sometimes when you hear that word, your mind goes to pretest with paper and pencil. Glad to see that this can be a true alternative. In your case, it showed you just where you needed to start your instruction, and it didn't take hours of grading to figure out.

—Erin (Colleague)

I love the idea of using these cubes to help assess where our students are in their learning. This proves to be a fun way to use preassessment rather than pretesting and standardized activities.

—Tina (Colleague)

I also love the idea of using the cubing as preassessment! What a great way to have the students involved in a variety of ways. We can spice up the activities to get the info we need.

—Sharon (Colleague)

It worked wonderfully. You are right about the conversations. I actually think I learned as much, if not more, from listening and jotting down notes than from the actual answers produced. The students are also not as "canned" with this type of preassessment.

—Tamra (Teacher)

SIMPLE MACHINES CUBE

Created by Deborah Gaff

Analysis
You have to move 1,000 kg. You need to have an MA of 20. Which machine is easiest to construct to move the object? Explain.

Synthesis
Design a compound machine with at least eight steps and two different simple machines that will break a balloon.

Application
Demonstrate mathematically how each of the six machines can provide a mechanical advantage.

Comprehension
Describe six items you use or see every day in terms of the six simple machines (e.g., scissors are two levers and two wedges).

Knowledge
List six simple machines.

Evaluation
Examine levers and a pulley system. What is the tradeoff for increasing mechanical advantage?

Real Teacher Comments

My class is using the cube to review simple machines. The synthesis activity is to design the Rube Goldberg apparatus. I think the biggest attraction for students was working towards something that seemed really cool—the building activity. Showing mastery of the first three activities led to a perceived reward.

—Deborah Gaff (Teacher)

Resources for Technology

Created by James Gasaway

Describe
List at least five different synthetic materials.

Persuade
Write a letter to persuade your boss why the company should or should not use a particular resource.

Associate
Choose one of the Young Hoosier books you've read so far and describe how a character interacted with specific tools and/or forms of energy.

Analyze
Create a poster that informs people about a particular form of energy.

Compare
Choose two tools from the table and compare their similarities and differences as machines.

Apply
Classify the various sources of energy as renewable or nonrenewable.

Real Teacher Comments

Probably because they had never experienced the cube before, students didn't treat it very seriously. Besides throwing the cube around, many students had trouble writing answers with as much depth and detail as they usually do when performing work from more traditional sources (like assignments posted on the overhead).

However, I think with experience, they will understand that the cube isn't any different than the way we have done questions or activities in the past.

—James Gasaway (Teacher)

I also had this experience until I became firm about the rules. When I use my firm voice, the whole class sits up and takes notice! I'm glad I don't have to use it very often. But after they realized this was an assignment and not a toy, they too began to work on it with more effort.

—Debra (Colleague)

The Activity Cube

Ask a question that will clarify something you might not understand regarding this sense.

Give an example of an illusion that relates to this particular sense.

Explain what the absolute threshold is for this particular sense.

Identify a stimulus of this particular sense.

Identify the receptor(s) for this particular sense.

What effects does this particular sense have on the way that we perceive our environment?

Created by Erin Goney

The Sense Cube

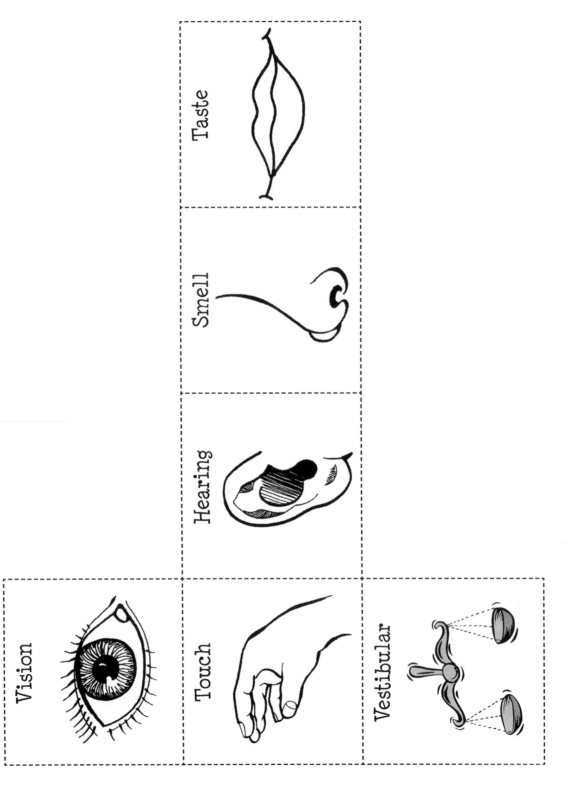

Vision

Taste

Smell

Hearing

Touch

Vestibular

Differentiation That Really Works: Science (Grades 6–12) © Prufrock Press Inc.

Real Teacher Comments

I decided to create a pair of cubes as a way to review for the sensation and perception unit that I am creating for this class. The students rolled both cubes, one to get the sense and the other to get the questions. I really enjoyed thinking of ways to create this type of activity, as we are always looking for new ways to review material with our students.

—Erin Goney (Teacher)

Anatomy and Physiology Cubing Activity
Digestive System and Metabolism: Biological Tier

Created by Heather Hall

Analyze
Create a chart that compares the digestive system of an invertebrate and a human.

Apply
Illustrate the human digestive system and show where and what type of bacteria inhabit the digestive tract. Explain the role of each in the digestive process.

Understand
Make an informational brochure that explains what *Heliocobacter pylori* are and what they cause. Include pictures.

Remember
Find a digestive system condition of any domestic vertebrate and tell how it is treated. Make a fact sheet about this.

Evaluate
Write a letter for a scientific journal explaining how a vestigial organ, the appendix, may have evolutionary implications.

Create
Design a digestive system that you feel would be most efficient. Tell what kind of organism (real or imaginary) would possess it. Explain its parts and function in a 3-D model.

Anatomy and Physiology Cubing Activity
Digestive System and Metabolism: General Tier

Created by Heather Hall

Remember

Make a fact sheet that defines the six essential activities of the gastrointestinal tract.

Understand

Sketch and label all organs of the digestive system. Indicate a condition that results in a homeostatic imbalance for four of the organs.

Apply

Write a story from the perspective of a piece of food entering a mouth. Tell the story of your journey from ingestion to excretion.

Analyze

Create a mobile showing the major organs of the human digestive system and the hormones involved in the action of each.

Evaluate

Conduct an investigation on fad diets. Find one and evaluate it in terms of its ability to sufficiently meet necessary nutritional needs.

Create

Produce a PowerPoint presentation that explains the effects and possible causes of obesity.

Anatomy and Physiology Cubing Activity
Digestive System and Metabolism: Medical Tier

Remember
Make a fact sheet about emesis. What is it? Why does it occur?

Understand
Construct a flip chart showing the role of hormones in digestion. This chart should include the source, stimulus for secretion, and action.

Apply
Write an article for the *Journal of the American Medical Association* explaining how jaundice can be a sign of gallstones.

Analyze
Compare the functioning of the small intestine with microvilli present and the functioning of the small intestine in the absence of them. You may choose any format for presenting your findings.

Evaluate
Research three different treatments for obesity. Create a postcard describing the benefits and side effects for each. Evaluate which one you, as a healthcare professional, would recommend.

Create
Produce a PowerPoint presentation that describes a congenital defect of the digestive system. Explain treatments for each.

Created by Heather Hall

Anatomy and Physiology Cubing Activity
Digestive System and Metabolism: Sports Medicine Tier

Remember

Make a chart. What is a nutrient? List the major groups and give examples of them.

Understand

Create a brochure. What is BMR? What factors affect it? How does each factor impact it?

Apply

Calculate your body mass index (BMI). Would you be considered obese? Explain.

Analyze

Graph the types and amounts of electrolytes contained in three different sports drinks. Which one would you recommend? Why?

Evaluate

Write an article for the school newspaper, *Chaos*, convincing high school athletes never to try anabolic steroids. Explain how steroid use is detrimental.

Create

Conduct research and create a diet that meets dietary needs of specific type of athlete, such as marathon runners, weight lifters, or swimmers.

Created by Heather Hall

Real Teacher Comments

I have spent more time on this strategy than on any of the others by far! I like this one a lot. I teach anatomy and physiology to juniors and seniors in our high school. I have found that the students fit into one of about four interest groups. The one-size-fits all approach does not seem to fit with them at all!

I have created this activity based on the four categories that the students usually fit into: those interested in some aspect of sports medicine, those interested in the medical field, those interested in the biological sciences, and those who don't have a specific interest. I designed this with the varied interests of those groups in mind.

—Heather Hall (Teacher)

These are great activities. I think that I could adapt some of them for use in my own human body unit. I am sure that high school students will enjoy the change of pace and the chance to create meaningful projects.

—Megan (Colleague)

As a secondary teacher, I can see students being engaged in your cubes. The statements you use are not as intimidating as what is often used in the course. Just the title of "anatomy" can sound scary.

—Tracy (Colleague)

Earth Science Review

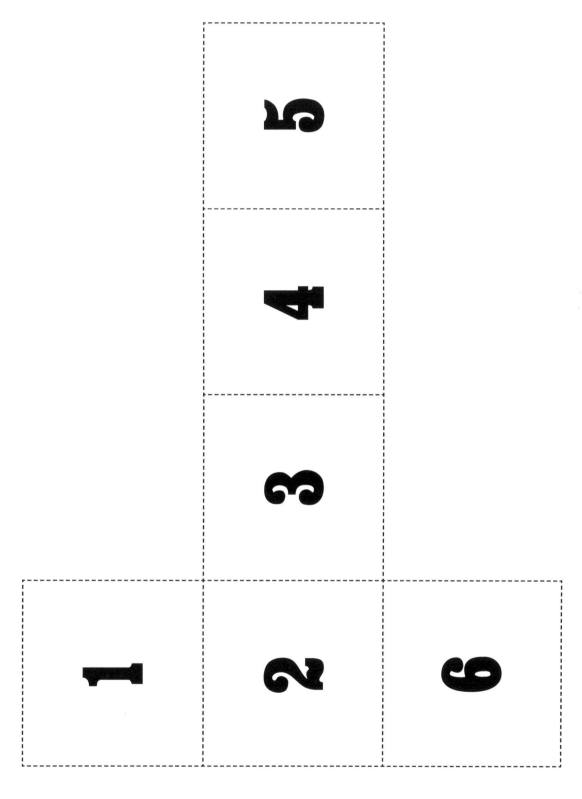

1

2

3

4

5

6

Earth Science Review

Plate Tectonics

LOWER LEVEL	HIGHER LEVEL
1. **List** the clues that support the theory of continental drift.	1. **List** the types of forces that cause the three types of faults.
2. **Explain** why some partly molten material rises towards Earth's surface.	2. **Explain** how the ages of rocks on the ocean floor support the theory of seafloor spreading.
3. **Organize** the types of boundaries, forces, and faults into a chart.	3. **Summarize** what properties of iron-bearing minerals on the seafloor support the theory of seafloor spreading.
4. **Compare and contrast** how plates move and transform boundaries by drawing diagrams with directional arrows.	4. Using a world map, **determine** what natural disasters might occur in Iceland and Tibet. Make a T-chart.
5. **Sketch** how continents fit together when they were connected in Pangaea.	5. Based on Activity #4, **speculate** why some Icelandic disasters are not expected to occur in Tibet.
6. **Infer** where the continents might be in one million years.	6. **Infer** why one plate subducts when two oceanic plates converge.

Earthquakes

LOWER LEVEL	HIGHER LEVEL
1. **List** the three types of faults.	1. **List** the types of faults and demonstrate how they move.
2. **Explain** and demonstrate how primary, secondary, and surface waves move.	2. **Explain** the differences between the three types of seismic waves and how they move.
3. **Summarize** how a tsunami is formed.	3. **Summarize** tsunamis—how they form and travel and why they are so devastating.
4. **Compare and contrast** normal/reverse/strike-slip faults.	4. **Compare and contrast** the number of deaths and the magnitude of earthquakes. Use an Internet search.
5. **Speculate** what it would be like if you were in a house where liquefaction happened.	5. **Speculate** why so many more people died in the 2003 earthquake (6.6 magnitude) in Bam, Iran than did in the 1994 earthquake in Northridge, CA (6.8 magnitude).
6. **Decide** what you would do in case of an earthquake here at school. Explain why you would do this.	6. **Decide** what you could do to make this classroom safer during an earthquake.

Volcanoes

LOWER LEVEL	HIGHER LEVEL
1. **List** the types of volcanoes.	1. **List** two important factors that control whether a volcanic eruption will be explosive or quiet.
2. **Describe** '*A'ā*, pahoehoe, and pillow lava.	2. **Explain** the relationship between the type of lava and the type of volcanic eruption.
3. **Categorize** the types of volcanoes, lava, and eruptions in a chart.	3. **Summarize** why magma cools quickly when it is forced out of a vent on Earth's surface.
4. **Compare and contrast** the three types of volcanoes.	4. **Compare and contrast** the types of intrusive igneous rock formations by creating a picture chart.
5. **Speculate** why most volcanoes form at divergent boundaries.	5. **Speculate** what would happen to the temperature of the Pacific Ocean if the Ring of Fire increased activity by 50%.
6. **Infer** why people would choose to live near volcanoes.	6. In 1883, Krakatau in Indonesia erupted. **Infer** which kind of lava Krakatau erupted— lava rich in silica, or lava low in silica. Support your inference using data.

Created by Vickie Linehan

Real Teacher Comments

I have created tiered cubing reviews to be used after each section of our Earth science unit. I have chosen to number the cubes so they can be used for multiple activities. The corresponding activities are on laminated sheets.

I have used cubing activities in the past. This activity will be used as a review for a comprehensive eighth-grade Earth science unit that will cover change within the Earth as observed through plate tectonics, earthquakes, and volcanoes.

—Vickie Linehan (Teacher)

I really like the format of your cubing activities. I am very impressed with how you've tiered the activities. I am working on Earth science now, and I can use your same concepts and modify the activities for my class.

—Julia (Colleague)

The different levels are easy to see, and both levels cover a large range of information and understanding.

—Allison (Colleague)

I like the level of detail. Great idea to make this a flexible activity that can be changed depending on your curriculum. It would also be easy to change from year to year with your different classes.

—Quella (Colleague)

SCIENTIFIC NOTATION

Created by Abby Meyer

ASSOCIATE

Name three branches of science that use scientific notation on a daily bases. Give an example for each one.

PROBLEM SOLVE

Iowa and Illinois are the top corn-producing states. In 2000, farmers in Iowa grew 1,740,000 bushels of corn, and farmers in Illinois grew 1,669,000 bushels. Write their combined corn production in scientific notation.

DISCUSS

Find a friend in the room; discuss how many different scientific notation equations you can come up with that relate to an amusement park. Try to come up with at least five.

EVALUATE

Create four problems in standard form and give the answers in scientific notation. Then create four different problems in scientific notation and gave the answers in standard form.

EXPLAIN

What are advantages of writing a number in scientific notation over writing it in standard form? Explain any disadvantages.

SUMMARIZE

In your own words, explain what the difference is between a number written in standard form and a number written in scientific notation.

Real Teacher Comments

I used this cube as a part of a scientific notation lesson. Writing numbers in scientific notation and standard form are sometimes confusing for students. Once we had discussed the process, worked some examples in class, and found some activities on the Internet, I used this cube as a way to determine students' level of understanding about scientific notation.

—Abby Meyer (Teacher)

I like the activities on your cube because they went beyond giving students a list of standard numbers to convert to scientific notation and vice versa. You could really get a good snapshot of each student's level of understanding.

—Tina (Colleague)

INVENTOR CUBE

YOU ARE THE INVENTOR

List the characteristics a person would need to be a good inventor, and explain your reasoning.

Find out about three men and three women who have invented something in the last 25 years.

List at least five items you think should be invented.

YOU ARE THE INVENTOR

Draw a picture of a new car you have just invented.

Think about the car's:
- shape,
- color,
- size, and
- windows.

Explain what an inventor does.

YOU ARE THE INVENTOR

You have invented something no one has ever seen or invented before. What is it?

Draw a picture of your invention. Name your invention.

Explain why you invented it.

Created by Erin Nolan–Higgins

Real Teacher Comments

For my first self-made cubing experience, I produced a cube on inventors and inventions to extend a lesson. For this first experience, we used the cube together. The group is very verbal, so it did lead to more questions.

The inventor cube led to two more sessions. The students liked having some control over the next activity and seemed to enjoy the different drawing activities. I found that giving them an overview of what they were going to do was a good start. Repeating the next steps as they continued seemed to help them. It is funny that these students can tell a story using as much description as a seasoned storyteller, yet putting it on paper is still a challenge.

—Erin Nolan-Higgins (Teacher)

I really liked your questions and prompts on your cube. They were all very open ended, which I am sure led to a variety of responses.

—Ashley (Colleague)

I liked the activity on the cube where students had to come up with an invention and explain why they had invented it. I'll definitely have to use that sometime. I also have some kiddos who can tell a great story, but their writing doesn't always reflect that.

—Mandy (Colleague)

I just completed my "Innovative Inventions" unit, and this is a great addition to my activities.

—Jennifer (Colleague)

Ecosystems Activities

Choose a biome and describe its characteristic abiotic factors, plant life, and animal life.

Give an example of a keystone species and describe what happens if that species is removed from the ecosystem.

Contrast the flow of energy with the flow of materials in an ecosystem.

Organize these from largest to smallest: population, organism, community, biome, ecosystem, and biosphere. Explain your reasoning.

Should wildfires in national parks be allowed to burn? State your opinion and support it with scientific information.

Create a food web with **at least** two producers, two primary consumers, and three secondary consumers.

Created by Deborah Price

Real Teacher Comments

I used this with my freshman biology students. We are reviewing content from the first semester in preparation for the end of course exam, and I thought the cube would be a fun way to review. Each student had to complete at least two sides in the 30 minutes I had allotted.

They were slow to get started, but once they did, it worked well. They seemed to like the change of activity. I had the students work and write their answers down so I could know who did what and could also correct any misconceptions or incorrect information that appeared. The side about the keystone species gave them some trouble, so I know that is something I will need to review again with the whole class.

—Deborah Price (Teacher)

This looks like a great cube. You have some quality activities for the students to do. For freshmen, I think they should be able to complete two sides in 30 minutes.

—Rachel (Colleague)

Great way to review. I like how you could determine what needs to be reviewed in greater detail from student responses.

—Dawn (Colleague)

I like the way you used this as a review! This is a much more fun way than just writing out answers or filling in a study guide. It's also a quick way to see what students need more review on and gives quick feedback.

—Kelly (Colleague)

Speed, Time, Motion, and Distance

Created by Allison Shakinis

Create
a story problem that can be used to graph motion.

Draw
a diagram showing the relationship between speed and time.

Define
speed, time, and motion so that an elementary student could understand the concepts.

Identify
what the variables are in the equation to solve for speed.

Evaluate
the distance from here to the end of the classroom, using the equation for distance.

Explain
how time and speed are related.

Real Teacher Comments

I had my students use the cube the day before our science test as a review. I assigned partners and then one student would shake the cube for his or her partner, who had to complete whichever activity the cube landed on. Students were told to do three different sides of the cube each, which meant that each pair would complete the whole cube. They really enjoyed this, and because they had to keep rolling until they came up with the new side, the repetition of repeating the other sides was great!

—Allison Shakinis (Teacher)

What I liked most about the science cube was its simplicity. It's great to have all of the colors and pizzazz when you have time—but the bottom line is that we all find ourselves more and more often in the position of having not enough time and pressing deadlines—it's nice to remember that simple can still be very, very effective.

—Sherri (Colleague)

I love the idea of using the cube for test review! I also like how you used the different levels of thinking. I can see using your cube as a template, keeping the verbs but changing the content for different units.

—Barbara (Colleague)

I love that you used it as a review, too! It will definitely be a way that I will use it in the future. And I really like how it could easily be changed up to go along with various subjects and topics.

—Rachel (Colleague)

Cellular Chemistry

Directions: Use your knowledge, note cards, journal, and book to complete the following:

1. Roll the cube and complete the activity shown.
2. Roll the cube at least two more times.
3. Record your responses in your journal, and then place your journal in the "Please Check" basket.

Remember
Identify each of the four organic compounds by its monomer and polymer.

Understand
Explain how the shape of an organic molecule determines its role in a cellular process.

Apply
Sketch the effect that a change in temperature or acidity will have on an enzyme.

Analyze
Use a Venn diagram to compare cellular respiration and photosynthesis.

Evaluate
Discuss why the concentration of common cellular molecules would differ between a muscle cell and a skin cell.

Create
As a group, design a cell membrane. Explain the structure and function for each molecule in your model.

Real Teacher Comments

It is that time of year when a review of first-semester material should help with end of course testing. I designed my cube to review organic compounds — specifically, how structure and the function of a molecule are related. I am curious to see if my high school students like the cube. For now, this review cube will be set up for students to try when they finish work early, a pleasant alternative to vocabulary note cards or reading an article.

Well, I tried the review cube today. Students reacted as I thought they would. Most students were glad to have a new way to do work. But after a couple of rolls of the cube, students just picked their activities by looking over all of the options and choosing the ones they wanted to do.

Overall, I think students like making the cube, and students like the choice of what review questions to do. So I see merit in trying this activity again. I could see making a cube for the major biological elements. Each student could study the name, symbol, and atomic number of each element in a random way.

Students completed three sides of the cube in 40 minutes. After reviewing their responses, I know that they need a little more help with enzyme function.

—Dawn Slein (Teacher)

Thinking About Pollution

List
List five kinds of pollutants and give an example of each.

Explain
Explain the impact of pollutants on the health of animals (including humans) and plants. Think! Provide details to support your answer.

Compare
Compare habitat destruction to pollution of the habitat. How are they the same? How are they different?

Infer
Describe what you think the world will be like in the future if the air pollution is not reduced.

Summarize
Summarize how water pollution is changing our fresh- and salt-water ecosystems.

Create
Create a new ending to the pollution problem on Earth. How do you imagine humans will solve the problem? Be sure to provide details and reasoning for your response.

Created by Deb Smith

Real Teacher Comments

I wanted to create an activity that would help my students bring together the information they've learned about pollution. I tried to use a variety of levels of Bloom's taxonomy so that students could reach beyond the knowledge level. By using higher level thinking skills, students could show me the depth of their understanding.

—Deb Smith (Teacher)

I like the fact that your cube got at higher levels of thinking. It underscores the importance of having students show what they know, understand, and are able to do beyond just knowledge and comprehension. I really liked your "create" activity. Maybe one of your students will be able to solve the pollution problem.

—Tom (Colleague)

CHAPTER 5

GRAPHIC ORGANIZERS

Overview

Graphic organizers are visual tools used by teachers to assist students in analyzing, interpreting, and making sense of the content. Graphic organizers come in many forms, depending on the use. Examples include Venn diagrams, compare/contrast charts, double bubble diagrams, and flow charts. Graphic organizers can be used as advanced organizers, sense-making activities, or as formative or summative assessments.

How and When to Use Graphic Organizers

Graphic organizers often are used as advanced organizers at the beginning of a lesson or activity to assist students in understanding the content. They also may be used for practice with activities that require students to make sense of the content. The teacher might choose to use graphic organizers to gather formative or summative data. To accommodate the needs of all learners, some organizers may be blank, while others may be partially completed, depending on the readiness level of the students.

Directions for Making Graphic Organizers

Graphic organizers are simple to design. However, there is no set template. The form and function of the graphic organizer will depend on the topic being taught, as well as the thinking skills students will be using. Inspiration®

is one type of software that can be used to create graphic organizers (http://www.inspiration.com).

How This Strategy Fits in the CIRCLE MAP

When used for assessment purposes, graphic organizers fit in the "differentiated assessment" component of the CIRCLE MAP. However, when used as an advanced organizer or sense-making activity, they fit in the "differentiated instructional strategies" component.

Examples

The examples we have chosen include specific graphic organizers, as well as those that can be readily adapted to many topics. These organizers were created by real teachers who used them in their own classrooms. When possible, we have included the comments from the teachers and their colleagues with the intention that the comments may provide additional insight to using the organizers.

For example, in Dr. Alexander's AP Physics class, the students are reviewing Newton's laws. He wants to use a graphic organizer to assist the students in distinguishing among the three laws. He plans to have the students design their own graphic organizers. The organizers must list the number of the law (e.g., Newton's first law), provide an alternate name (e.g., the law of inertia), explain what it states (e.g., the velocity of an object remains constant unless acted upon by a force), and give an example (e.g., if a moving car stops suddenly, the passengers will continue to move forward unless stopped by seatbelts). Students design and complete the graphic organizer while Dr. Alexander walks around the room to get a good idea of which students seem to have mastered the concept and which students might still need some reteaching. Once the students have completed their graphic organizers, he has them share their work.

Template

Due to the nature of graphic organizers, there is no universal template.

Compounds Graphic Organizer

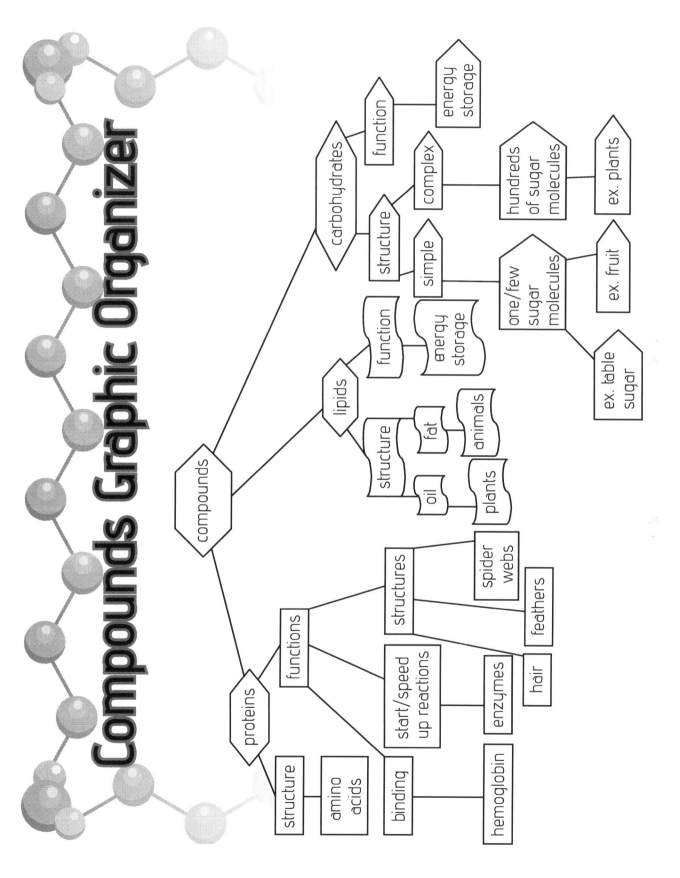

compounds

carbohydrates
- function — energy storage
- structure
  - complex — hundreds of sugar molecules — ex. plants
  - simple — one/few sugar molecules — ex. fruit — ex. table sugar

lipids
- function — energy storage
- structure
  - fat — animals
  - oil — plants

proteins
- functions
  - structures — spider webs — feathers — hair
  - start/speed up reactions — enzymes
- structure — amino acids
- binding — hemoglobin

Real Teacher Comments

This is the organizer we created to show the connections for the interactions created by the body when food is eaten. The students still struggle with organizational webs. Many of them have trouble seeing connections. They like it when the organizers are completed and the connections are obvious. I try to use these often with students, especially when I have a large number that have trouble recognizing connections.

I like to use a variety of graphic organizers in lessons. I also like to have the students create their own for a variety of situations. This works especially well after they have had plenty of opportunity to use a variety.

—Tamra Cargile (Teacher)

Exploring Convection

Convection: the transfer of energy from place to place by the motion of heated gas or liquid.

So what does that mean to me?

Lab Time

Let's see convection in action!

Carefully record your observations so you can apply your understanding in new ways.

Convection in my heating system?
Convection in a city or forest?
Convection at the shore?
Convection under water?
What does "catch a thermal" mean?

Created by Deborah Gaff

Exploring Convection

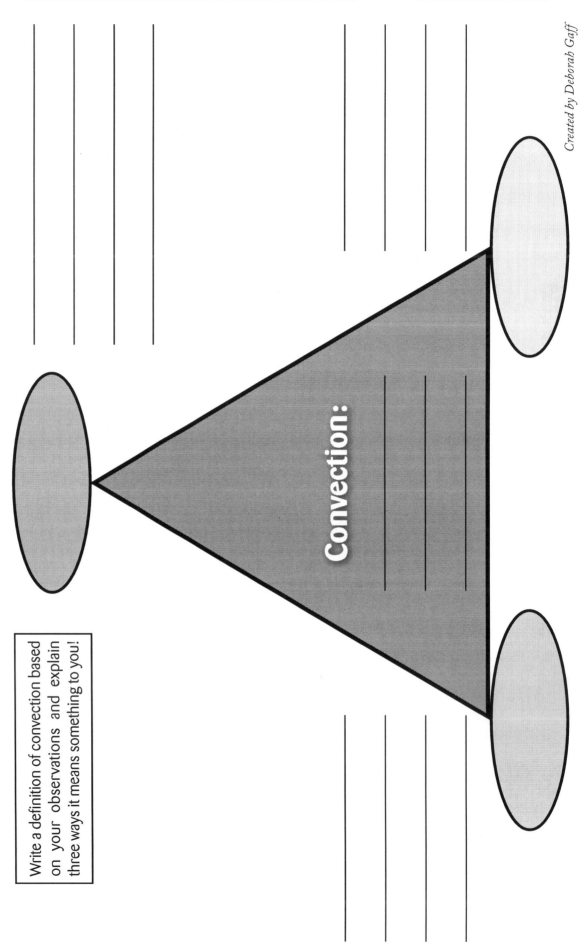

Convection:

Write a definition of convection based on your observations and explain three ways it means something to you!

Real Teacher Comments

I am working on breaking the habit students have of just memorizing the textbook definitions. The students often do not know what the definitions mean or how they can use them in everyday life.

This organizer is two pages. The first page I shared on the overhead with the entire class. I copied the textbook definition as an introduction to the lab, and then we did a lab to get a better understanding of the definition. The application questions were given in advance so that students had a focus for their learning. I heard great "ah ha" moments when students made observations during the lab that helped them answer application questions.

As part of the lab packet, students were given illustrations to go along with each of the questions and were asked to draw the convection lines. The second page of the graphic organizer asked them to put the definitions into their own words and to give three examples. I even got examples that I did not ask for—one student put "convection oven" and remarked that she always wondered what they were.

—Deborah Gaff (Teacher)

Cranial Nerves
Flipbook Example

The front of each flap would contain the following:

Nerve name:	Illustrated clue for function:
1. Olfactory	
2. Optic	
3. Occulomotor	
4. Facial	
5. Glossopharyngeal	
6. Vestibulocochlear	
7. Vagus	
8. Hypoglossal	

The back of each flap would contain the following:

Nerve origin:	Function:
1. Fibers arise from olfactory receptors in the nasal mucosa and synapse with the olfactory bulbs.	Purely sensory; carries impulses for the sense of smell.
2. Fibers arise from the retina of the eye and form the optic nerve. The two optic nerves form the optic chiasma by partial crossover of fibers.	Purely sensory; carries impulses for vision.
3. Fibers run from the midbrain to the eye.	Supplies motor fibers to four of the six muscles that direct the eyeball.
4. Fibers leave the pons and run to the face.	Activates the muscles of facial expression and lacrimal and salivary glands; carries sensory impulses from the taste buds of the anterior tongue.
5. Fibers emerge from the medulla and run to the throat.	Supplies motor fibers to the pharynx that promote swallowing and saliva production.
6. Fibers run from the equilibrium and hearing receptors of the inner ear to the brain stem.	Purely sensory; vestibular branch transmits impulses for the sense of balance and cochlear branch transmits impulses for the sense of hearing.
7. Fibers emerge from the medulla and descend into the thorax and abdominal cavity.	Fibers carry sensory impulses from and motor impulses to the pharynx, larynx, and abdominal and thoracic viscera.
8. Fibers run from the medulla to the tongue.	Motor fibers control tongue movements; sensory fibers carry impulses from the tongue.

Created by Heather Hall

Real Teacher Comments

I like to use flipbooks in class—especially in anatomy, where there is so much vocabulary. Flipbooks are made by staggering sheets of paper, folding them over, and stapling them. Sometimes the students like to use different colors of paper on their flipbooks.

This is an example of a flipbook that students could create for the cranial nerves. (My list is not complete in the example I gave.) I created mine on the computer; however, I usually have the students do theirs by hand.

The specific cranial nerve is listed on the front, and a visual clue is included that relates to the function of that nerve. The flaps are cut in the middle. On one side of the flap is the origin of the nerve, and on the other side is the function. I have found many different ways to use flipbooks. The students seem to enjoy them and find them useful.

—Heather Hall (Teacher)

I like using flipbooks too or foldables. Your graphics were good for the flipbook; they would help the kids remember the words.

—Sharon (Colleague)

This is a really neat idea! I like how you've set it up and would have the students create their own flipbooks. I could see using this in my classes when teaching vocabulary or grammar concepts or simply when reviewing for a test or exam. Very creative!

—Rachel (Colleague)

This seems like a great way to help your students learn difficult content.

—Megan (Colleague)

THE WORLD'S BIOMES

Created by Vickie Lineham

Describe each of the world's biomes.

Include climates and organisms.

The World's Biomes

Real Teacher Comments

Here is a graphic organizer I use for biomes. My students liked this because they could narrow down their pages of notes into one simple page. They will use this one-page organizer to create graphs about the precipitation and temperatures in various biomes.

—Vickie Linehan (Teacher)

CELL ORGANELLES

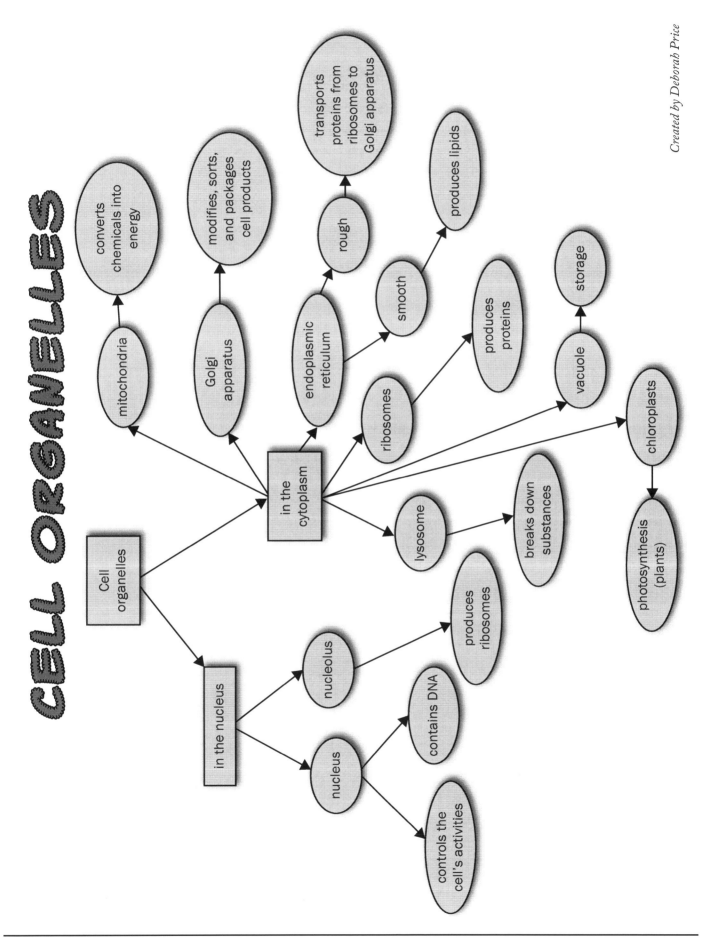

Created by Deborah Price

Real Teacher Comments

This is an organizer I created to help my students review cell organelles, their location, and their function. This was used for review for the upcoming state end-of-course exam. The location (nucleus or cytoplasm) was given, and students were to place the names and functions correctly. This was a good review activity, and the students liked doing it on the computer because it was easier to move things around and correct mistakes.

—Deborah Price (Teacher)

Great web! I really like how that can organize information for students. The cell is never an easy concept for students, because you can't touch it or see it in a large perspective. It forces you to think beyond what is "normal" and apply skills to understand just how tiny a cell is and everything that is inside it.

What is great about this organizer is that students could keep elaborating on it and provide more details for each part of the cell. I've had my students relate the different parts of the cell to a city, so the mitochondria would be the power company. This organizer would allow you to continue to expand on it to include more information. The only thing I would add to this organizer is some color. Because it is packed full of great information, I think it would be easier to follow with different paths by using a different color for each part.

—Robert (Colleague)

This is a fun way to revisit cell organelles!

—Dawn (Colleague)

Photosynthesis
Concept Map

Use the terms to complete the concept map and the equation below.

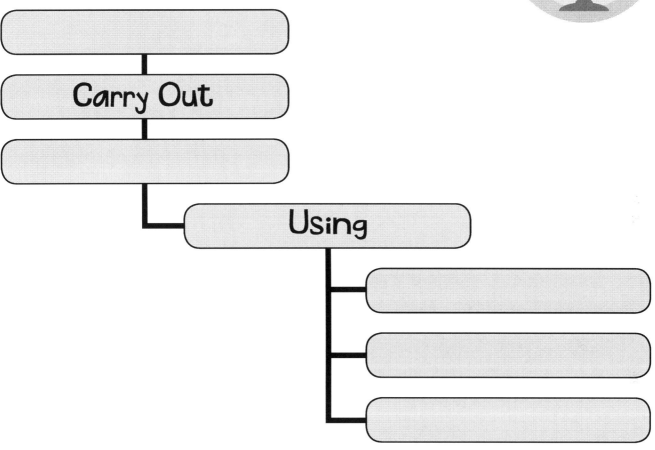

Carry Out

Using

Water
Photosynthesis
Plants
Carbon Dioxide
Light Energy

_____ + Water + _____ = Glucose + _____

Light Energy
Oxygen
Carbon Dioxide

Created by Allison Shakinis

Respiration
Concept Map

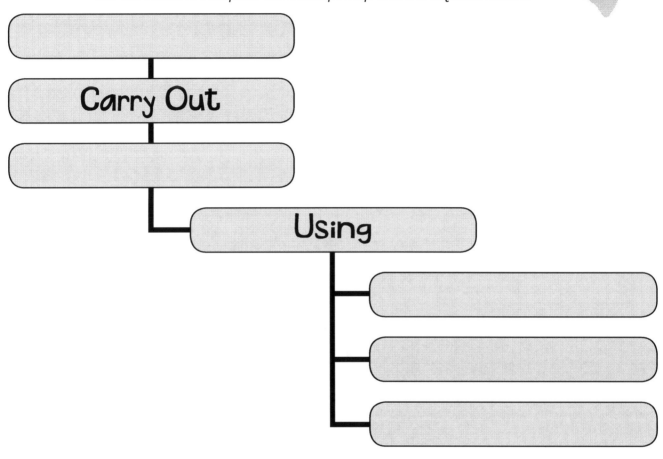

Use the terms to complete the concept map and the equation below.

Carry Out

Using

Water
Respiration
Animals
Carbon Dioxide
Energy

Glucose + _____ = _____+ Water + _____

Energy
Oxygen
Carbon Dioxide

Created by Allison Shakinis

Real Teacher Comments

The graphic organizer I created is one that deals with photosynthesis. I also created a second organizer that deals with cellular respiration. Both of these were put on an assignment together to help the students understand their differences and how they are interconnected.

The students did well filling these out. A few struggled with figuring out the first word in the concept map and in the future I may have that added already.

—Allison Shakinis (Teacher)

One of the things I've noticed, both as a teacher and as an administrator, is how challenging note taking is for our students—regardless of grade level. This type of partially filled-in format is an excellent way to guide students on how to take notes, target the main ideas, and so on.

—Sherri (Colleague)

Types of Reproduction

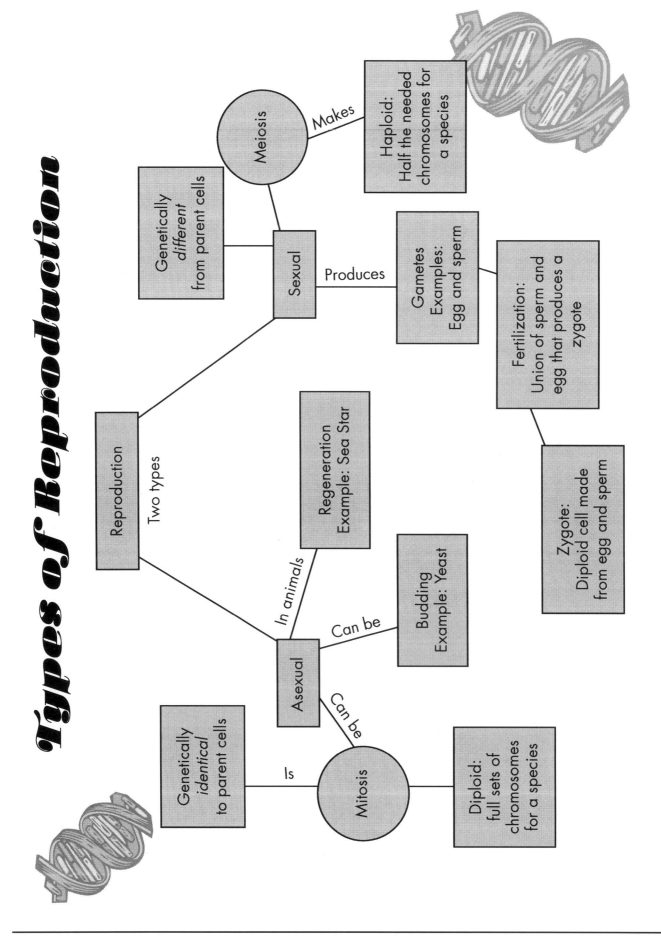

Reproduction

Two types

Sexual
- Genetically different from parent cells
- Meiosis — Makes — Haploid: Half the needed chromosomes for a species
- Produces — Gametes Examples: Egg and sperm
  - Fertilization: Union of sperm and egg that produces a zygote
  - Zygote: Diploid cell made from egg and sperm

Asexual
- In animals — Regeneration Example: Sea Star
- Can be — Budding Example: Yeast
- Can be — Mitosis
  - Is — Genetically identical to parent cells
  - Diploid: full sets of chromosomes for a species

Created by Dawn Slein

Real Teacher Comments

All of my classes use graphic organizers of various types in every unit we study. We start the organizer as a class, and then each student finishes independently. They construct the organizers in their journals, on quizzes, or as a review exercise. Overall, biology students find organizers to be difficult to do. But by the end of the year, they realize that if they know the material, the organizer is easier to make.

My eighth-grade students are not as familiar with using and constructing their own concept maps. Consequently, we have constructed them as a class most of the year. Slowly, they have been expected to finish more of the concept maps on their own. We just started a new unit, and a preassessment indicated that many students had a good understanding of the beginning material. We used the 10-word vocabulary list for the beginning of the unit to construct a map of what students already knew about reproduction. I started the map on the board with the word "reproduction," and then students worked in pairs using dry-erase boards to construct a map of the words they were confident that they knew.

Then, as a class, we constructed a map that included sketches and connecting words for each line. We defined each word using the book definition and using our own words. Students copied the class map in their journals. They "kept score" on the accuracy of the maps they had made on their individual boards. We added new vocabulary (e.g., haploid, diploid) and discussed what DNA had to do with reproduction. My students came up with the idea to use the same shapes or colors for similar processes and terms.

—Dawn Slein (Teacher)

I just take for granted that my students understand how to use an already-constructed graphic organizer. With all of this information, I can see where it would be beneficial for your students to be able to create their own organizers—what a great study skill they can use over and over in each class. Some classes are so complicated that it is difficult for kids to be able to organize the information, and really, this is a perfect way to teach them to simplify their process.

—Kelly (Colleague)

I think that it is great that you are teaching the students how to use the graphic organizers, both together as a class and individually. This is a great study tool for students to learn to use across all curricular areas. It sounds like you give students a lot of control over their learning and have developed an effective learning community where all students are benefiting from the concept maps and graphic organizers!

—Rachel (Colleague)

My first thought was that I wish I'd had a teacher in high school who did this with my class! The students may not like doing it at the beginning, but hopefully they will learn to appreciate this skill that you are teaching them.

—Jenna (Colleague)

Name:_____ **Date:**_____

GRAPHIC ORGANIZER FOR
LIFE CYCLE OF A STAR PROJECT

Note: Remember to name each required stage that you are going through and write the essential details that you experience. You may need more or fewer boxes to complete your life cycle than located here. You may use more than one box for a stage if needed.

#1. Determine if you are a low-mass or a high-mass star. Life cycles are different.

#2. How do you form? Name the stage and provide essential details.

#8.

#3.

#7.

#4.

#6.

#5.

Created by Deb Smith

Real Teacher Comments

I have found that a graphic organizer is a good way to have students keep track of the elements of a project. Students have to pretend they are a star and explain all of the processes involved in their life cycle. To ensure that they have the appropriate level of detail, I provided some prompts in the beginning boxes. Some students need the prompts, and some do not. This is one of my students' favorite activities.

—Deb Smith (Teacher)

I teach biology, and I can easily adapt this organizer when we discuss the life cycles of various living things. Even some of my brightest students need assistance with organizing the various parts of a cycle. I'm sure my students will enjoy this graphic organizer. Thanks for the great idea.

—Tina (Colleague)

Kinematics

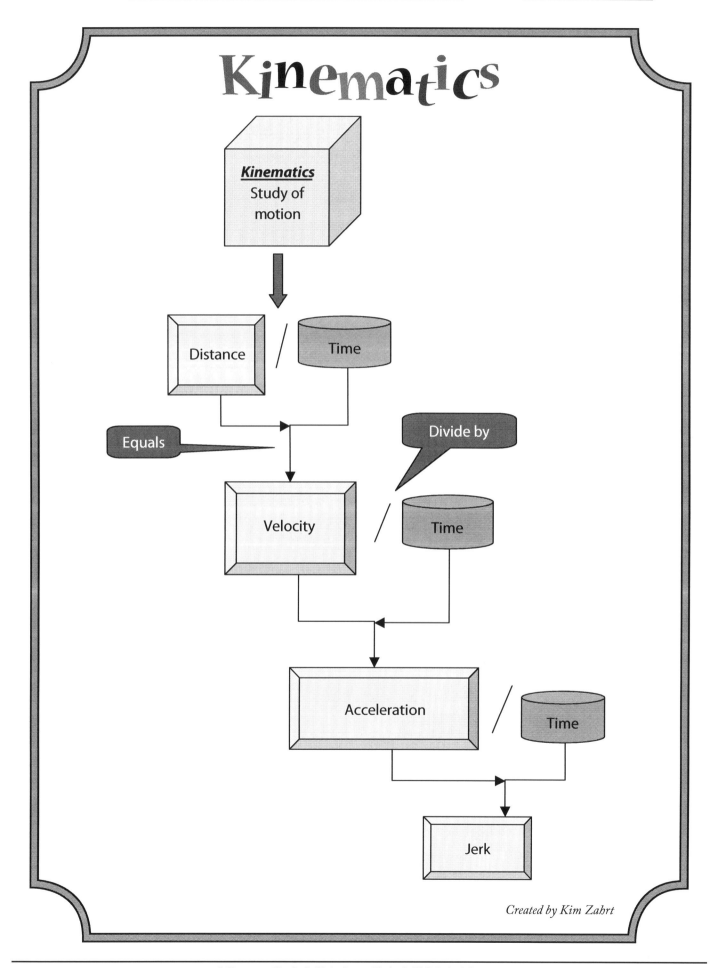

Real Teacher Comments

One of the subjects first taught in physics is kinematics. I've created a simple graphic organizer that shows the students the relationship of distance, velocity, acceleration, and jerk. When I give this to the students, I remove the words and have the students fill it in. It can also be used as a pretest.

—Kim Zahrt (Teacher)

I like your idea of using the graphic organizer as a pre- and postassessment. I am going to use this with my students. Thanks for the great idea.

—Jeri (Colleague)

This graphic organizer is really interesting. I like how you represent the calculations in an easy-to-read visual flow. I have experience with Inspiration™, but limited access to it. I have never seen it used this way.

—Erin (Colleague)

Visually, I really like the use of the speech balloons for annotations/labels. They make it very clear that this is not part of the diagram, but rather is a note to help the students understand the symbols. I also think using this as a pre- and postassessment is a great idea, and one I will try myself.

—Lisa (Colleague)

After seeing how you put your organizer together, I think I will use a similar one in my seventh-grade science class. I never thought of using a flow chart/ web combination (alteration) to show computational relationships. Thank you for sharing.

—Tamra (Colleague)

CHAPTER 6

LEARNING CONTRACTS

Overview

Learning contracts are "bargains" between the teacher and a student or group of students. Learning contracts may be on any topic and may be considered abbreviated lesson plans or mini-units. That is, learning contracts list standards, concepts, goals, activities, resources, products, and assessments in a format that is student-friendly. They have a starting and ending date and a place for the student, the teacher, and the student's parents to sign indicating that the contract is binding. Generally, learning contracts are used as an alternative to regular instruction, especially when students have been compacted out of a portion of the curriculum.

How and When to Use Learning Contracts

In a classroom, the learners are at a variety of readiness levels. To accommodate these differences, many teachers begin a unit of instruction by pre-testing the entire class on the planned content. Some students already may know significant portions of the content and need alternative activities while the rest of the class proceeds with learning the content that is new to them. To provide clearly articulated learning experiences for the students who already have mastered the planned content, a learning contract often is an appropriate choice. Generally, the student and teacher jointly plan the contract, agree to the terms, and sign it. In our experience, it also is vital that parents sign the contract to avoid unnecessary miscommunication.

Directions for Making Learning Contracts

Learning contracts are simple to create using the template provided below. However, it is easy to design your own learning contract customized to a particular topic. Any learning contract should include all of the elements of the template.

How This Strategy fits in the CIRCLE MAP

A learning contract fits in the "differentiated instructional strategies" component of the CIRCLE MAP. Learning contracts are generally alternative assignments used to accommodate individual or small-group rather than whole-class learning needs.

Examples

The examples we have chosen all use the template but address different topics. These contracts were created by real teachers who used them in their own classrooms. When possible, we have included the comments from the teachers and their colleagues with the intention that the comments may provide additional insight to using the learning contract and for creating your own or another topic.

For example, Sam, Libby, and Thai are students in Laura Dawson's honors seventh-grade life science class. The class was about to begin studying microorganisms. On a pretest over that topic, Mrs. Dawson found that most of her class had only rudimentary knowledge about types of microorganisms. The exceptions were Sam, Libby, and Thai. All three scored 97%–100% on the pretest and indicated a positive to very positive attitude towards the topic. She met with the three students to discuss possible options for a learning contract for them to use during the time the other students would be working through the unit. These students were very interested in studying the topic in greater depth and wanted to be able to do so with a hands-on approach. Although labs would be conducted with the whole class, these students wanted to access labs that required a deeper understanding than what was expected in the regular curriculum. Mrs. Dawson helped the students identify books, videos, and websites that would be helpful. She keyed the objectives to the state standards and developed the contract, making sure to include checkpoints to ensure that the students were on target with their independent work. Once developed, each contract was signed by the student, his or her parents, and Mrs. Dawson.

Template

Title of Learning Contract

Standards:

Goals/Objectives:

Topic:

Activities:

Resources:

Product/Outcome:

Evaluation Criteria:

Signatures:

Student: _____   Date: _____

Teacher: _____   Date: _____

Parent: _____   Date: _____

Science Fair Project
Learning Contract

Name: _____

Start Date: _____   **Due Date:** _____

Subject: Science

✿ ✿

Standards:

- Design investigations, use computers and other technology to collect and analyze data, explain findings, and relate investigations to science as a whole.
- Recognize and explain that hypotheses are valuable, even if they turn out not to be true, if they lead to fruitful investigations.
- Select tools, such as cameras and tape recorders, for capturing information.
- Organize information in simple tables and graphs and identify relationships they reveal.
- Use tables and graphs as examples of evidence for explanations when writing essays or writing about lab work, fieldwork, and so on.
- Locate information in reference books, back issues of newspapers and magazines, CD-ROMs, and computer databases.
- Analyze and interpret a given set of findings, demonstrating that there may be more than one good way to do so.
- Recognize and describe that the results of similar scientific investigations may turn out differently because of inconsistencies in methods, materials, and observations.
- Begin to evaluate the validity of claims based on the amount and quality of the evidence cited.
- Keep a notebook to record observations and to be able to distinguish inferences from actual observations.
- Use technology, such as calculators or spreadsheets, in determining area and volume from linear dimensions. Find area, volume, mass, time, and cost, and find the difference between two quantities of anything.
- Write instructions that others can follow in carrying out a procedure.
- Read and follow step-by-step instructions when learning new procedures.
- Recognize when and describe how comparisons might not be accurate because some of the conditions are not kept the same.

✿ ✿

❀❀❀

Learning Goals and Objectives:

1. Students will design, conduct, and present their findings of a scientific investigation to their classroom and in the school's science fair.
2. Students will demonstrate an understanding of, and accurately apply the scientific method to, their investigation, planning, and implementation.
3. Students will collect accurate and detailed data and observations.
4. Students will draw reasonable conclusions based upon their evidence.
5. Students will effectively communicate their work and conclusions, both verbally and in writing.
6. Students will manage their time and resources effectively while working independently, both at home and school.

❀❀❀

Activities and Progress Checks: The following set of activities will guide you through the process of preparing a science fair project. When you have completed the activity at a certain step, write your initials in the box. Be prepared to present your completed work to your teacher at conferences on the dates of progress checks. At that time, your teacher will initial your contract if the work is satisfactory. If your work is time sensitive and you need to present work before the date of the progress check, make arrangements with your teacher to conference before the date.

Date of Progress Check	Activity Description	Student Initials	Teacher Initials
	1. Read and understand the Science & Engineering Fair Rules.		
	2. Create a guiding question that you would like to answer through your investigation.		
	3. Conduct research to learn as much as you can about the topic of your question; write a summary of your research findings.		
	4. Formulate a hypothesis and an investigation plan; describe your purpose, question, hypothesis, variables, controls, materials, procedure, and plan for data collection.		
	5. Collect all materials necessary to conduct your investigation.		
	6. Conduct the investigation.		
	7. Collect and analyze all data and observations; use Excel to create graphs and charts to effectively communicate your results.		

Differentiation That Really Works: Science (Grades 6–12) © Prufrock Press Inc.

Date of Progress Check	Activity Description	Student Initials	Teacher Initials
	8. Create a published (typed) report in which you describe your investigation, your results, your conclusions, and your reflections.		
(FINAL DUE DATE)	9. Prepare your science fair exhibit with evidence and a display board that presents your information (with a title, abstract, and pictures and descriptions of your purpose, problem, hypothesis, variables, materials, and conclusion—and if they fit, descriptions of your data and procedures).		
	10. Practice speaking confidently about your work and answering questions.		
	11. On the due date, bring everything for your presentation, including the following: ___ Display board ___ Published report with a summary of your research ___ Actual data and observations collected ___ Evidence or examples (according to the rules)		

Student's Guiding Question:

____

____

Resources:

1. Society for Science and the Public website (http://www.societyforscience.org): Find lots of resources, tips, advice, and information about writing an abstract.
2. Science fair resources in the classroom
3. Library: You will have multiple opportunities to conduct research in the school library and will need to conduct more research at your neighborhood IMCPL branch.
4. Internet: You will have access to the classroom computer.
5. Mentors: We will work with you to find a mentor working in a profession that relates to your topic.

Product/Outcome:

1. You will be expected to present your work, speak confidently about your investigation and conclusions, and answer questions from others.

2. To supplement your presentation, you will also need to include an exhibit with the following:

   ● ___ Display board (with a title, abstract, and pictures and descriptions of your purpose, problem, hypothesis, variables, materials, and conclusion—and if they fit, descriptions of your data and procedures)

   ● ___ Published report with a summary of your research

   ● ___ Actual data and observations collected

   ● ___ Evidence or examples (according to the rules)

Signatures: Once the student decides upon his or her guiding question, the student and parent must sign below. After reviewing the student's question, the teacher will also sign the learning contract. By signing, all agree to the expectations established above.

Student: _____   Date: _____

Parent: _____   Date: _____

Teacher: _____   Date: _____

Created by Jamilyn Bertsch

Real Teacher Comments

In past years, participation in the school's science fair was optional for sixth graders. This year, as a part of our International Baccalaureate curriculum, we are requiring all of our students to participate. Those with a great deal of experience will not need as much support as some of my other students. Thus, I have developed this learning contract to guide the learning for those experienced students who will be working on the process independently.

I know that the students (and the parents especially!) will appreciate the detailed list of activities with scheduled dates for progress checks. In the past, they were given a very basic contract that required very little accountability, and because it was optional, some students who signed up did not fully accomplish the task. I think that this learning contract will help each student avoid getting lost in the process and create a more highly developed science fair project.

—Jamilyn Bertsch (Teacher)

Learning Contract:
SCIENCE GRADE 7

Name: _____

Start Date: _____ **Due Date:** _____

Science Standard:
- Recognize and explain that heat energy carried by ocean currents has a strong influence on climates around the world.

Goals/Objectives: Demonstrate a greater technical understanding of ocean currents and how ocean currents have impacted exploration and travel.

Topic: Ocean Currents

Activities: Answer the following questions using the following website: http://www.oar.noaa.gov/k12/html/enrich_currents2.html.
1. Research the different types of sailing vessels used by traders in the 1500s through the 1900s. How did the materials used to build the vessels change? How did the sails change? How did the navigation change?
2. Research "doldrums" and "horse latitudes." Why are these areas named this way?

Resources:
- World maps
- Poster board for timeline
- Links provided at the website above

Assessment: The students must submit:
1. an illustrated timeline of changes in sailing vessels from the 1500s through the 1900s, which includes details about materials and sails;
2. a map of three significant trade routes used during colonial times; and
3. a three-paragraph paper explaining the doldrums and horse latitudes.

Signatures:

Student: _____

Parent: _____

Teacher: _____

Created by Deborah Gaff

Real Teacher Comments

We are studying about ocean currents and climate, and I had four students who already had advanced knowledge of the topics. I developed the learning contract so they could demonstrate a great understanding of ocean currents and how they affect exploration and travel. The students were engaged throughout the whole learning contract timeline and produced projects that indicated that they had gained advanced understanding. They presented their work to the rest of the class to share their findings.

—Deborah Gaff (Teacher)

I liked the simplicity of your contract. I plan to have my students study this topic in a few weeks and hope to use your contract as it is or modify it slightly for my advanced students.

—Tom (Colleague)

Name: _____

Start Date: _____   **Due Date:** _____

Subject: **Anatomy and Physiology**

Standard: **Have a working knowledge of the functions of cells and their organelles.**

Goals/ Objectives: **The student will focus her attention on an area of interest to her. She is interested in cancer research. She will demonstrate her knowledge in a presentation.**

Topic: **Cell Biology**

Activities:
★ **Because she achieved a score indicating mastery in cell biology, it will not be necessary for this student to work through the unit on cell organelles with the rest of the class. Instead, she will create a PowerPoint presentation that will be given to the class.**
★ **Arrangements will be made for her to visit the Jasper County Hospital oncology department.**

Directions: **Research current treatments in cancer and specifically target five different chemotherapeutic drugs used in the treatment of cancer. How do they impact the cell and its organelles and the process of mitosis? Based on your findings, evaluate which you feel is most suited for the treatment of cancer. Explain your viewpoint.**

Resources:
★ *Essentials of Human Anatomy and Physiology* **(textbook)**
★ *Journal of the American Medical Association*
★ **Internet sources**
★ **Local hospital's oncology department**

Product/ Outcome: **PowerPoint presentation given to class**

Evaluation Criteria: **A rubric will be used to evaluate the presentation. This will be presented to and discussed with the student prior to the start of the project.**

Signatures:

Student: _____

Parent: _____

Teacher: _____

Created by Heather Hall

Real Teacher Comments

I created this learning contract for a student who I have had in class previously. We did something similar, but I was unaware of learning contracts at that time. I also recently added the visit to the oncology department. I really need to find more opportunities to take advantage of the use of the hospital, which is our high school's next-door neighbor.

—Heather Hall (Teacher)

What a great idea to use a community site for helping advanced learners do more authentic research. You've helped remind me that there are many untapped resources in my own community, and I plan to make more of an effort to include them for my students.

—Tina (Colleague)

LEARNING CONTRACT

NAME: _____

SUBJECT: _____

START DATE: _____   DUE DATE: _____

STANDARDS:
- Explain that humans help shape the future by generating knowledge, developing new technologies, and communicating ideas to others.

GOALS/ OBJECTIVES:
- ⮱ Describe how people predicted and explained earthquakes in the past.
- ⮱ Describe how scientists predict and explain earthquakes today.
- ⮱ Hypothesize how scientists might predict earthquakes in the future.

STUDENTS WILL KNOW:
- ⮱ How seismic waves travel through the different layers of the Earth.
- ⮱ How the epicenter of an earthquake is calculated.
- ⮱ How a seismograph works.
- ⮱ How earthquakes are measured.

STUDENTS WILL UNDERSTAND:
- ⮱ Different ways people predicted earthquakes in the past.
- ⮱ Different ways people explained earthquakes in the past.
- ⮱ How earthquakes are predicted today.
- ⮱ How earthquakes are explained today.
- ⮱ The relationship between the epicenter and the focus of an earthquake.
- ⮱ How technology used to measure and predict earthquakes is constantly changing.

STUDENTS WILL BE ABLE TO:
- ⮱ Research the history of earthquake explanations and predictions.
- ⮱ Compose an essay that outlines the history of predictions from ancient to present and incorporate possible future prediction techniques.
- ⮱ Design a brochure or earthquake-prediction kit.
- ⮱ Prepare and deliver an oral presentation (with visual aids) that outlines the history of earthquake explanations and predictions.

STRATEGIES:
- ⮱ Read various texts about past predictions and explanations of earthquakes.
- ⮱ Research through the Internet.
- ⮱ Write and/or compose.
- ⮱ Create a brochure or advertisements with Microsoft Publisher.
- ⮱ Give an oral presentation.

TOPIC/CONCEPT: The ways in which earthquakes are explained and predicted have changed over time and are continuing to change as new technology is developed.

ACTIVITIES:

- ❧ Students will read about the history of seismomography.
  - Students will read about the history of seismomography.
    - The Earth: Who Invented the Ancient Chinese Earthquake Detector?
      - o http://www.enotes.com/science-fact-finder/earth/who-invented-ancient-chinese-earthquake-detector
    - Who Invented the Seismograph?
      - o http://inventors.about.com/od/sstartinventions/a/seismograph.htm
    - The Early History of Seismometry (to 1900)
      - o http://earthquake.usgs.gov/learning/topics/seismology/history/history_seis.php
- ❧ Students will read about how ancient people explained earthquakes.
  - Earthquake Myths and Legends
    - o http://www.chevroncars.com/learn/wondrous-world/earthquake-legends
  - Earthquake Myths and Folklore
    - o http://www.ceri.memphis.edu/aware/myths.html
- ❧ Students will read about current explanations of earthquakes.
  - Elastic-Rebound Theory of Earthquakes
    - o http://www.sciencedaily.com/articles/e/elastic-rebound_theory.htm
- ❧ Students will read about past earthquake-prediction techniques.
  - Earthquake Prediction Using Earthquake Clouds
    - o http://www.indiaref.net/articles/earthquake-prediction-using-earthquake-clouds
  - Animals and Earthquake Prediction
    - o http://earthquake.usgs.gov/learning/topics/animal_eqs.php
  - Can Animals Sense Earthquakes?
    - o http://news.nationalgeographic.com/news/2003/11/1111_031111_earthquakeanimals.html
- ❧ Students will read about current earthquake-prediction techniques.
  - Earthquake Prediction
    - o http://www.pnsn.org/INFO_GENERAL/eq_prediction.html
  - Quake Prediction
    - o http://www.pbs.org/wnet/savageearth/earthquakes/html/sidebar2.html

- 🌀 Students may research the topics at other sites of their choosing.
- 🌀 Students will hypothesize how earthquakes might be predicted in the future by **writing an essay** that outlines the history of prediction from ancient to present and incorporates possible future prediction techniques.
- 🌀 Once students have read about past and present explanations and predictions of earthquakes, they will **design a brochure or earthquake-prediction kit.** The brochure or prediction kit may focus on any of the following:
  - the history of earthquake explanations (ancient to present),
  - the history of earthquake predictions (ancient to present), or
  - the future of earthquake predictions.
- 🌀 They will use their product as part of an <u>**oral presentation**</u> on the history of earthquake explanations and prediction (ancient to present).

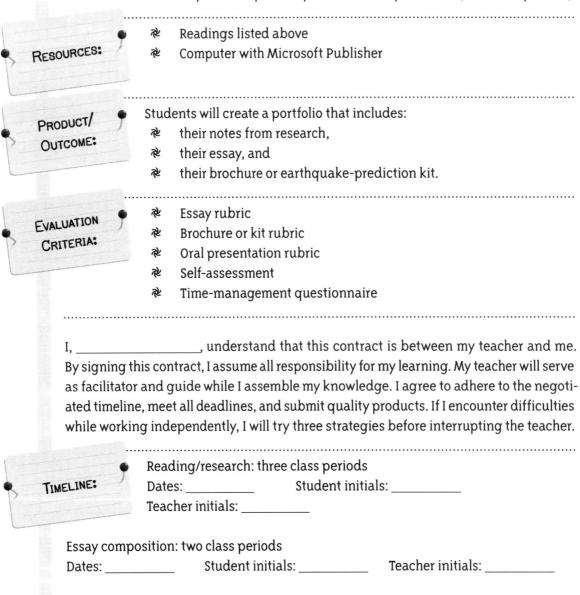

RESOURCES:
- 🌀 Readings listed above
- 🌀 Computer with Microsoft Publisher

PRODUCT/ OUTCOME:

Students will create a portfolio that includes:
- 🌀 their notes from research,
- 🌀 their essay, and
- 🌀 their brochure or earthquake-prediction kit.

EVALUATION CRITERIA:
- 🌀 Essay rubric
- 🌀 Brochure or kit rubric
- 🌀 Oral presentation rubric
- 🌀 Self-assessment
- 🌀 Time-management questionnaire

I, _____, understand that this contract is between my teacher and me. By signing this contract, I assume all responsibility for my learning. My teacher will serve as facilitator and guide while I assemble my knowledge. I agree to adhere to the negotiated timeline, meet all deadlines, and submit quality products. If I encounter difficulties while working independently, I will try three strategies before interrupting the teacher.

TIMELINE:

Reading/research: three class periods
Dates: _____   Student initials: _____
Teacher initials: _____

Essay composition: two class periods
Dates: _____   Student initials: _____   Teacher initials: _____

Brochure/kit design: three class periods

Dates: _____   Student initials: _____   Teacher initials: _____

Rehearsal for presentation: one class period

Date: _____   Student initials: _____   Teacher initials: _____

Oral presentation: one class period

Date: _____   Student initials: _____   Teacher initials: _____

All final products are due on presentation day:

Date: _____   Student initials: _____   Teacher initials: _____

SIGNATURES: STUDENT: _____

PARENT: _____

TEACHER: _____

Created by Vickie Linehan

Real Teacher Comments

My eighth-grade earth science class is composed of the entire range of learners, from struggling to advanced, with this particular content. Our textbook gives basic information about earthquakes and their prediction. I wanted to provide a learning contract for my advanced learners so they could study the topic in depth. I also wanted them to use a historical perspective as they gained new knowledge. When the students shared their projects with the class, the other students were fascinated by the various ways earthquakes had been predicted over time.

—Vickie Linehan (Teacher)

I liked the idea of the historical perspective with earthquakes. The last time I taught this topic we focused on basic information as well as incidents of recent earthquakes. Based on your work, I will add the historical focus next I teach this topic.

—Kyle (Colleague)

Learning Contract:
Sixth-Grade Science

Name: _____

Start Date: _____   **Due Date:** _____

Standards: Human activities have changed the capacity of the environment to support some life forms.

Goals/Objectives: The student will test and gather information on the water pollution around industrial sites, sewage plants, medical facilities, and public landings in two local creeks. The student will have a control water sample value from the Department of Natural Resources and the local water plant. The student will take all gathered information and create a pamphlet to present at city council. This pamphlet will contain at least one graph of the data collected and one picture. The student will present the findings at the local city council and give recommendations to help in the improvement of any areas found to be substandard.

Topic: Pollution: The Silent Killer?

Activities:
1. Take water quality readings three times at each location.
2. Take water quality readings on three different dates.
3. Interview members of the local fishing and sports club about the changes in the quantity and quality of fish they catch.
4. Interview the local Department of Natural Resources.
5. Interview the local water treatment plant manager.
6. Interview two to three families who live along one of the creeks.
7. Contact the Environmental Protection Agency.

Interviews will include questions on noted changes in the flora and fauna in the area and the type and number of fish that are caught, as well as information on the health of fish caught, such as weight.

Student will be taught the proper procedures and will use the proper precautions to keep safe and free from contaminants.

Resources: Computer, Internet, EPA, DNR, local fishing and game organizations, local ecological organizations, public records, textbook, and water quality records

Product/Outcome:

▶ Produce a pamphlet that will explain what, if any, local pollution from various locations is causing the number and quality of flora and fauna to decrease.

▶ Make recommendations to local city councils on what areas need to be monitored and/or cleaned up for improvement of water quality.

Evaluation Criteria: Student will be evaluated on the proper completion of the pamphlet. The pamphlet must contain at least one graph and one picture. All information in the pamphlet must be documented. Student must be able to present pamphlet with understanding and confidence.

Signatures:

Student: _____

Teacher: _____

Parent: _____

Principal: _____

Created by Cynthia McKee

Differentiation That Really Works: Science (Grades 6–12) © Prufrock Press Inc.

Real Teacher Comments

I have several students who have a great interest in the effects of pollution on living things and who have already shown mastery on the pollution unit in our textbook. I designed this learning contract with the students and with support from their parents because students will need to be transported to some of the locations. Because we have a block schedule, students will be able to gather their data at a particular location and still return in time for their next class.

—Cynthia McKee (Teacher)

I think it is great that you have parents who are willing and able to get students during the day to take them to the various locations. Most of my students' parents work and would not be able to transport them during the day. However, we have a number of locations nearby where students could gather data, and I could modify your learning contract slightly to take this into consideration.

—Tina (Colleague)

Body Systems
Learning Contract

This contract replaces the regular class work for the body systems of mammals. Your signature indicates your agreement to complete all work as specified.

Name: _____ **Grade:** 12 **Subject:** AP Biology

Start Date: _____ **Due Date:** _____

AP Biology Themes: Relationship of Structure to Function; Regulation; Science, Technology, and Society

Standards: Structure and Function of Plants and Animals

Goals/Objectives: At the end of the learning contract, students will:
- know the important organs of the human body and their locations,
- understand how the structure of the organ affects its function,
- apply that knowledge to a medical situation,
- describe how disease affects organ function in various body systems, and
- use the knowledge of healthy body function to educate others.

Activities: Read all directions before you begin.
1. Label the organs and structures in the packet using correct medical terminology. (A good website that can be used for finding the organs and structures is http://web.jjay.cuny.edu/~acarpi/NSC/14-anatomy.htm.)
2. Complete the medical case study in the folder. (A website where you can locate an appropriate case is http://sciencecases.lib.buffalo.edu/cs/collection/about.asp.)
3. Research a disease of your choice and write a paper detailing how the disease affects different body systems. The paper is to be typed, double-spaced, and minimum three pages. A properly formatted resources list is required.
4. Create a presentation for first graders that will inform them about a health issue. The presentation should influence the children to make healthy choices. The presentation should be 15–30 minutes in length.

Resources:
- ➤ AP Biology textbooks
- ➤ Anatomy manuals and books
- ➤ Internet sources for research (be sure to use reliable sources)
- ➤ Computers

Product/Outcome:
- ➤ Students will turn in
  - ___ Diagrams packet
  - ___ Case study
  - ___ Research paper

- ➤ Students will present to the class
  - ___ Health presentation for first graders

Evaluation Criteria: Students will be evaluated based on:
- ➤ their correct labeling of the packet;
- ➤ their solution to the case study and their explanations for this solution;
- ➤ the quality of information in their research paper, the quality of writing, and the correct format for a research paper; and
- ➤ the quality of information in their health presentation and the appropriateness of the presentation for the intended audience.

Signatures:

Student: _____

Teacher: _____

Parent: _____

Created by Deborah Price

Real Teacher Comments

This learning contract is for my AP Biology students who are planning a career in the health field. The activities are centered on the medical profession. I plan to create other learning contracts for the rest of the class, emphasizing different aspects of animal structure and function. These will be based on student interest and ability.

—Deborah Price (Teacher)

Great idea for students interested in the medical field! I really like how you incorporated younger students for an audience. It would be a nice addition if students were actually able to share their work with a class of first graders.

—Dawn (Colleague)

—— Learning Contract ——

Subject: Science

Start Date: _____   **Due Date:** _____

Standards:
- ◆ Identify some important contributions to the advancement of science, mathematics, and technology that have been made by different kinds of people in different cultures at different times.
- ◆ Investigate that an unbalanced force acting on an object changes that object's speed, path of motion, or both and know that if the force always acts toward the same center as the object moves, then the object's path may curve into an orbit around the center.

Topic: Gravity: A Force of Attraction

Goals/Objectives: By completing the following activities, I will be able to describe gravity and its effect on matter, along with explaining the law of universal gravitation. I will understand why Sir Isaac Newton realized that gravity existed.

Activities: (Check each off as it is completed. Complete the activities in order!)

_____ Meet with your teacher for a minilesson on gravity. (A website that has information you can use for this topic is http://www.sciencenetlinks. com/lessons.php?DocID=390.)

_____ Research Sir Isaac Newton on a reliable Internet source or encyclopedia, and type a one-page, double-spaced paper on the discoveries that Newton made.

_____ Research the unusual characteristics of Io and Europa, two of Jupiter's moons. Create a poster that shows the effects of Jupiter's gravitational force on the moons and explains why scientists think Europa may have life forms.

_____ What is the difference between weight and mass? What can you use to measure weight? What can you use to measure mass? Write out your answers.

_____ Write a reflection about what you learned through these activities. In it, address any new questions that you have.

Resources:
- ◆ Computer
- ◆ Internet Explorer

Product/Outcome: After completing these activities, I will have a better understanding of what gravity is and how it works. I will be able to explain it using my own words and examples from different sources.

Signatures:

Student: _____

Teacher: _____

Parent: _____

Evaluation Criteria:
- ◆ All activities should be completed.
- ◆ Each individual activity will be graded.

Created by Allison Shakinis

Real Teacher Comments

I used this learning contract for various students who have been identified as high ability. We are covering a unit on force and motion, using science kits that are available at our school. I decided to extend some of the content to students who are high ability. This content is added into the learning contract.

The students so far have enjoyed checking off what they have completed. They were at home for a few extra days over fall break, and one of them completed the entire thing, which was great to see!

—Allison Shakinis (Teacher)

I really liked the structure of your learning contract and that each activity was to be done in order. It almost seems like it was a minilesson within the contract. I could see myself using a contract more along these lines with my students as well.

—Rachel (Colleague)

LEARNING CONTRACT

Name: _____   **Subject:** General Biology

Start Date: _____   **Due Date:** _____

References check: _____

Interview date (if conducting an interview): _____

Visual aid choice
(options are PowerPoint, poster, flyer, or video): _____

Your suggestion must be approved by the teacher: _____

Progress check: _____

Standards:
▶ Describe the consequences of introducing non-native species into an ecosystem, and identify the impact this may have on that ecosystem.
▶ Recognize and describe how human beings are part of Earth's ecosystems. Note that human activities can, either deliberately or inadvertently, alter the equilibrium in ecosystems.

Goals/Objectives: While others are completing assignments about population growth, you can complete an Invasive Species project. This research project allows you the option to research population size, how it changes, and the limiting factors that influence these changes. Then you will consider the impact that a non-native species can have on the environment. Additionally, you will consider how human activity can alter an ecosystem. Consider your project to be a resource that will help other students to learn about non-native species.

Topic: Non-Native Species (Invasive Species)

Activities: A visual aid will be constructed in which you do the following:
▶ identify a non-native species in your state,
▶ explain how this species was introduced into your state,
▶ diagram the spread of this species through your state,
▶ discuss how humans can reduce the spread of the non-native species, and
▶ describe the impact this species has on the environment.

Resources:

- ▶ Internet sources about non-native species, population growth, and limits to population growth
- ▶ Your state's Department of Natural Resources for information about invasive species
- ▶ Classroom resources
- ▶ Local and regional newspaper articles

Product/Outcome: You will create a visual aid on a non-native species of your choosing. This may be a PowerPoint, a poster, a flyer, or a video.

Evaluation Criteria: A rubric will be provided based on the visual aid you choose.

I realize that I must work independently during biology class and not interrupt anyone. I must use my time and resources wisely.

Signatures:

Student: _____

Teacher: _____

Parent: _____

Created by Dawn Slein

Real Teacher Comments

I wanted to incorporate independent learning, and having a specific format gave me the courage to try it. I believe that independent learning is a skill. As you could guess, my students come with a wide range of independent learning skills. Many times, the high-ability students lack study skills. Because of this, a lot of the "teaching the skills" has to happen in the beginning for them. Another concern is about having equipment/supplies for independent learning. My vision for some independent study involves investigating and redesigning labs.

Instead of my long-term projects, I am considering setting up 3–5 independent study topics that students can choose from for each grading period. All students will have to complete one project per grading period. Additionally, students who need more challenge can be given independent options. Certainly, students could create their own topics (approved by me) that cover the state standards.

Overall, I believe students will enjoy the opportunity to work at their own pace. With guidance, each student can complete a project successfully. Hopefully, students with high apathy will begin to invest in learning a little more.

The invasive species independent study is a modified version of a long-term project.

—Dawn Slein (Teacher)

Name: _____ **Date:** _____

Learning Contract

Name: _____ **Subject:** Grade 7 Science

Start Date: _____

Progress Checks (as Needed): _____

Due Date: _____

Standards:
- Explain that viruses, bacteria, fungi, and parasites may infect the human body and interfere with normal body function. Recognize that a person can catch a cold many times because there are many varieties of cold viruses that cause symptoms.
- Explain that white blood cells engulf invaders, produce antibodies that attack invaders, or mark the invader for killing by other white blood cells. Know that the antibodies produced will remain and can fight off subsequent invaders of the same kind.

Goals/Objectives:
- Students will be able to explain that specific pathogens, such as bacteria and viruses, cause diseases in humans that interfere with normal body functions.
- Students will be able to explain how the immune system fights infections.

Topic: Viruses, Bacteria, and Diseases

Activities:
1. Find out about bacteria and viruses.
2. Find out how diseases are spread and how your immune system works.
3. Choose one bacterial pathogen and the disease it causes. Research this disease using the Internet and classroom resources. Write a paragraph or two about this pathogen explaining how the pathogen is transmitted, the symptoms it causes, the duration of symptoms, the seriousness of the disease, and how the disease is prevented or cured.
4. Outline the steps your body takes when responding to a virus.

Resources: Reference materials, magazines, and Internet sources with diagrams of viruses, bacteria, antibodies, white blood cells, and the immune system

Specific Websites:

- American Lung Association Lung Disease Finder
  - o http://www.lungusa.org/lung-disease/finder.html
- CDC Influenza Prevention and Control
  - o http://www.cdc.gov/flu
- HowStuffWorks: How Your Immune System Works
  - o http://www.howstuffworks.com/immune-system.htm

Product/Outcome: You are a viral pathogen! Determine which viral pathogen you wish to be and research the details of the disease/symptoms it causes. Make a children's book, write a short story, create a PowerPoint presentation, or tape a song of your life as this pathogen. Tell us of your experiences traveling into the human body and of your adventures fighting against the human body's immune system.

Evaluation Criteria:

- Specific virus identified, as well as the symptoms it causes
- Prevention strategies discussed
- Method of transport and point of invasion identified
- Correct body responses given, along with details to invasion, in a logical order
- Prognosis given (do you die or infect someone else?)
- C.O.P.S. (correct capitalization, organization, punctuation, and spelling) on all written work
- WOW! Go above and beyond expectations

I realize I must work independently during science and not interrupt others. I must use my time and resources wisely. I understand that I should see my teacher if I do not understand the written directions or if I have any questions. I realize that I may need to wait until the teacher is available to ask my questions.

Signatures:

Student: _____

Teacher: _____

Parent: _____

Created by Deb Smith

Real Teacher Comments

My learning contract is for a unit on bacteria, viruses, and diseases. I have a few students each year who already know the information we cover in class on the basics of bacteria and viruses and need something a little different. We only briefly cover diseases in class and the body responses, so I chose this topic for the students to go into more depth on their own. The students have really enjoyed working on this contract and were eager to present their new knowledge.

—Deb Smith (Teacher)

I really liked the creative way you had students present what they had learned. Having them pretend to be a viral pathogen incorporated all of the vital information you wanted them to learn without them having to write an essay or take a test. I plan to try that with my next learning contract for advanced learners.

—Tom (Colleague)

CHAPTER 7

TIERED LESSONS

Overview

According to Adams and Pierce (2006), tiered lessons are designed for all students to address the same academic standard or concept, but at varying levels of depth, complexity, or structure. Tomlinson (1999) indicated that tiered lessons are staples for differentiating instruction. Tiered lessons allow several pathways for students to arrive at an essential understanding based on the students' readiness. Erickson (2002) described essential understanding as "the key principles and generalizations that develop from the fact base. . . . They are the 'big ideas' that transfer through time and across cultures" (p. 47). Implementing a tiered lesson implies that the teacher has a good understanding of the students' ability levels with respect to the lesson and has developed the tiers to meet those needs. The number of tiers depends on the range of ability levels in the classroom.

How and When to Use Tiered Lessons

Use tiered lessons anytime you need students to work on similar material but at varying levels of readiness. Readiness can be reflected in skill level, reading level, or ability to handle multiple sets of directions, for example. As we noted before (Adams & Pierce, 2006), many examples of tiered lessons have three tiers: below grade level, at grade level, and above grade level. There is no rule that states there may only be three tiers, however. The number of tiers depends on the range of ability levels in the classroom. Remember: You will be forming tiers based on the assessment of your students' abilities to handle the material particular to the lesson. Students are regrouped when you decide to move to a different lesson. The number of groups per tier will vary, as will the number of students per tier. Do not try to form groups of equal size; instead, groups should be formed based on the readiness needs of individual students. For example, Tier One may have two groups of three students; Tier Two may have five groups of four students; and Tier Three may have one group of two students. Even if students already are grouped into classes by ability, there is still variability at each ability level, and teachers still need to address these varied ability levels in each population. What you don't want to have happen is that students' tiers differ in the *amount* of work they have to do rather than the *kind* of work they do. Second, be sure each tier is doing moderately challenging and developmentally appropriate work. In other words, no group should be given "busy work." One group should not be doing blackline practice sheets, while another does a fabulous experiment.

Directions for Making Tiered Lessons

According to Adams and Pierce (2006), there are nine steps to developing a tiered lesson.

1. Identify the grade level and subject for which you will write the lesson.
2. Identify the standard (e.g., national, state, and/or local) that you are targeting. A common mistake for those just beginning to tier is to develop three great activities and then try to force them into a tiered lesson. Start with the standard first. If you don't know where you are going, how will you know if you get there?
3. Identify the key concept and essential understanding. The key concept follows from the standard. Ask yourself, "What 'Big Idea' am I targeting?" The essential understanding follows from the concept. Ask yourself, "What do I want the students to know at the end of the lesson, regardless of their placement in the tiers?"
4. Develop a powerful lesson that addresses the essential understanding. This will be the base from which you develop your tiers.
5. Identify the background necessary to complete the lesson and be sure students have this necessary information to be successful in the lesson. What scaffolding is necessary? What must you have already covered or what must the student have already learned? Are there other skills that must be taught first?

6. Determine which element of the lesson you will tier. You may choose to tier the content (what you want the students to learn), the process (the way students make sense out of the content), or the product (the outcome at the end of a lesson, lesson set, or unit—often a project).
7. Determine the readiness of your students. Readiness is based on the ability levels of the students. Preassessing is a good way to determine readiness.
8. Determine how many tiers you will need based on your assessment of the students' readiness to engage in the lesson based on its focus.
9. Determine the appropriate assessment(s) you will use based on your activities. Both formative and summative assessments may be included in the lesson. (pp. 21–22)

How the Strategy Fits in the CIRCLE MAP

Tiered lessons fit in the "differentiated instructional strategies" component of the CIRCLE MAP, as a whole-group activity. Tiered lessons accommodate a variety of readiness levels through whole-class instruction: All students work with the same standard and concept but follow different pathways leading toward the same essential understanding.

Examples

The examples we have chosen include lessons for specific topics and grade levels that may be readily adapted to other grade levels. These lessons were created by real teachers who used them in their own classrooms. When possible, we have included the comments from the teachers and their colleagues with the intention that the comments may provide additional insight into developing your own tiered lessons.

For example, Jack Nixon's AP Biology class is studying plant diversity. Mr. Nixon creates a lesson that focuses on transpiration under four different environmental conditions. The differences among the tiers will be the levels of critical thinking that must be employed. For example, some students will be working on activities that involve application and analysis, and others will work with synthesis and evaluation activities. While students are working on their activities, Mr. Jackson rotates from group to group to observe student progress and provide assistance as needed. Once all of the labs are completed, students engage in a class discussion to debrief the lab.

Template

Title of Tiered Lesson

Subject:

Grade:

Standard(s):

Key Concept:

Essential Understanding:

Background:

Tiered in Content, Process, or Product (choose one)

Tier I:

Tier II:

Tier III:

Assessment:

Applying Formulas

Subject: Science

Grade: 7

Standard:
　※　Use formulas to calculate the circumference, area, and volume of various shapes.

Key Concept: Formulas

Essential Understanding: Formulas can be used to find the two-dimensional or three-dimensional space that any shape occupies.

Background: We apply formulas as we do lab work throughout the year. Students have been studying the interactions between organisms and their environments. This lesson will give students a practical way to apply these formulas. Readiness is determined by previous observations and assignments involving these calculations.

Tiered in Content

　　Tier I: Students will be given the task of developing feeders that will fit in a space no larger than an area that is 40 cm x 40 cm x 40 cm and will hold the most feed for animals in a zoo habitat.

　　Tier II: Students will be given the task of designing a pool for dolphins that has three depths—1 m, 10 m, and 100 m—and holds 100kL of water. They must then decide if the tank is appropriate for dolphin performances. If they decide it is not, they must make a list of recommendations.

Assessment: The teacher will rotate among groups to monitor progress and give directions as needed. Final submissions will be evaluated for correct use of formulas.

Created by Tamra Cargile

Real Teacher Comments

I am grouping students into those who I have determined use formulas with ease and those who still struggle. At this time, I have no middle group for this skill. I seem to have a group that is distinctly divided in math skills. I will place students in groups of three or four depending on the number of students in the tier and the number present that day. I will then give the groups the task that is appropriate for them. I fully expect this to be a challenge for all students due to the level of thinking involved.

I try to incorporate many real-world problem-based learning activities. The students do enjoy learning much more that way. It sometimes takes a while for a few of them to warm up to actually not doing the easy book work, but once they do a few activities, they like this method better.

My students know from the beginning of the year that I do not have artistic ability, but I draw or diagram almost everything. By this time in the year, I have several students who automatically incorporate similar drawings into their own work. I also find that when they work in groups, they are more likely to include them.

My students loved this activity. Many asked if we could do these activities more often, and several wanted to construct models of their ideas. I was able to make many notes about the discussions and thought processes that were occurring during the lesson.

—Tamra Cargile (Teacher)

I like what you're asking of the kids in this lesson. It is a real-world problem, and I believe that kids just step up to the plate knowing that they are doing something other than a problem in a book. Asking the students to create a pool for dolphins seems very similar to many of the problem-based learning activities I have read.

—Sonny (Colleague)

I teach seventh-grade math to sixth-grade students. Our students are also in advanced science. I really like your lesson and would love to use it in my upcoming geometry unit as a cross-curricular lesson. My students are terrible at converting from standard units to metric units. One idea for Tier III is to have the students do the same thing as Tier II students but be required to submit their work with both metric and equivalent standard measurements, as we often buy construction materials using standard units.

—Anthony (Colleague)

Subject: Science

Grade: 8

Standards:
- ○ All students should develop an understanding of properties and changes of properties in matter, motions and forces, and transfer of energy.
- ○ In grades 5–8, students observe and measure characteristic properties, such as boiling and melting points, solubility, and simple chemical changes of pure substances, and use those properties to distinguish and separate one substance from another.

Key Concept: Acids and Bases

Essential Understanding: Students will be able to use an indicator to distinguish between acids and bases and place substances along an acid/base continuum.

Background: Discuss the taste and feel of common household products; how might that help us understand the properties related to acids, neutrals, and bases? For instance, lemon juice is sour, baking soda is bitter, lemon juice stings a cut, and soaps make a floor slippery.

Pretest: Students will identify common household products as acids, neutrals, or bases.

Tiered in Process

Tier I (Grade Level): Students will identify household products as acids, neutrals, or bases based on their reactions with cabbage juice as directed in the lab at this link: http://www.pcds.org/share/sci8/labs/cabbage.htm.

Tier II (Advanced): Students will place common items along a pH continuum using pH litmus paper and cabbage juice as directed in the lab at this link: http://mrskingsbioweb.com/labs/pH%20Experiment%20rev.pdf.

Assessment: Assessment is formative as students correctly identify acids and bases in Tier I and place common products along the pH continuum in Tier II. A rubric will be used for the lab report, and students will work with their lab partners to complete the lab.

Created by Deborah Gaff

Real Teacher Comments

I find that the lab activities described in the textbook are generally very basic and prescribed. I like to find hands-on activities for my students that they will find challenging and engaging. Unlike the textbook's activities, the activities I find don't show pictures of the completed product, making the results of the lab more dramatic and exciting for the students. I found that the web has great choices for most labs from my textbook.

—Deborah Gaff (Teacher)

I have taught science for many years and have been disappointed in the cookbook style that seems to be prevalent there. Students get a recipe and are shown the result. This eliminates higher level thinking and hypothesizing. I too have found great resources on the web.

—Sonny (Colleague)

Understanding Tsunamis

Subject: Science

Grade: 8

Standard: The Physical Setting

Key Concept: Earthquakes have the potential to be violent demonstrations of the change within the Earth and on Earth's surface. When the focus of the earthquake is under the ocean, it can cause a tsunami. In the open ocean, tsunamis appear as regular waves; however, as they come closer to shore and the ocean becomes shallower, the wave becomes a towering wall of water that slams into the shore with great force.

Essential Understanding: We can learn about tsunamis by studying past tsunamis and the earthquakes that caused them. We can further learn how seismic waves travel by studying how tsunamis travel.

Background: Students have background knowledge of tectonic plates—how they were created, where they are located, and how they move. They also know the different types of faults (normal, reverse, and strike-slip), the direction in which the crust moves at each of these faults, and the tension forces that cause the movement. Students have read about plate tectonics and earthquakes, have watched several videos about them, and have read Internet articles about them. Prior to this lesson, students will take a quiz about the bending and speed changes of seismic waves as they travel through different material, the validity and procedure of earthquake intensity measurement, and the effects of earthquakes. Based on quiz scores, students will be placed in two different groups.

Tiered in Product

Tier 1 (Basic): This group will investigate tsunamis—their causes, effects, common locations, frequencies, and any other information students deem important to understanding preparedness. Upon completion of individual research, groups will come together to

create word webs, using Inspiration™, to show the interrelationship of common terms.

Tier 2 (Advanced) This group will investigate tsunamis—their causes, effects, common locations, frequencies, and any other information students deem important to understanding preparedness. Upon completion of their individual research, groups will come together to create informational brochures that outline causes, effects, signs, and evacuation plans for tsunami survival.

Web Sources:
- ❖ National Geographic Tsunamis
  - o http://environment.nationalgeographic.com/environment/natural-disasters/tsunami-profile.html
- ❖ Geologic Hazards on the Oregon Coast: The Science of Tsunamis
  - o http://www.oregongeology.org/sub/earthquakes/Coastal/ScienceofTsunamis.htm

Assessment: Assessment will be formative as the teacher rotates through the group to listen to the discussion, correct any misconceptions, and make sure the group is on task. Rubrics will be provided to each group for product assessment.

Created by Vickie Linehan

Real Teacher Comments

This particular tiered lesson is very effective for both tiers of students. They seem to come away with a clearer understanding of tsunamis. The students particularly liked the websites, because they are authentic. I was pleased at the depth of information that students in Tier I used in creating their word webs. The brochures that students in Tier II created were exceptional and well planned.

—Vickie Linehan (Teacher)

Energy Within an Ecosystem

Subject: Science
Grade: 6

Standard:
- Recognize and explain that two types of organisms may interact in a competitive or cooperative relationship, such as producer/consumer, predator/prey, or parasite/host.

Key Concept: Energy

Essential Understanding: All living things need food and energy, but the types of food and energy consumed are not the same for all organisms.

Background: Students will have been introduced to and have knowledge of the following terms: predator, prey, consumer, producer, parasite, and host. Students will also understand the terms carnivore, herbivore, and omnivore.

Tiered in Product

Tier I: These students will draw or make a collage of a food web for a biome of their choosing and will label the predator, prey, consumer, producer, parasite, and host found in that biome.

Tier II: These students will make a menu for an herbivore, carnivore, and omnivore. At the top of each column, they will place a picture of a living organism that serves as an example of a carnivore, an herbivore, or an omnivore. In the menu, students will place food items for the herbivore, carnivore, and omnivore under categories of predator, prey, consumer, producer, parasite, and host.

Tier III: These students will select two herbivores, two omnivores, and two carnivores. The selection must be in pairs of predator/prey, producer/consumer, and parasite/host. For each organism selected, students will explain the different adaptations that the organism possesses to make it easy to get the type of food that organism eats. The students will produce a minibooklet demonstrating what they learned, to be placed on the science reading shelf.

Assessment: Students will be given a rubric for their final projects. These projects will be graded by the use of the rubric. Grading will also be ongoing as they work to complete their project.

Created by Cynthia McKee

Real Teacher Comments

The students in my sixth-grade science class run the whole gamut from learners who struggle with grade-level materials to those who are much more advanced in their understanding. Tiered lessons are a great way to take the same concept and understanding and provide different pathways for the students to demonstrate what they know, understand, and are able to do.

Based on a pretest, I placed the students in one of three tiers. All of the students were able to complete the work assigned to their tier, and no one seemed out of place as they completed the work. Students were absorbed in the project throughout. The students who usually struggle were able to successfully complete the food web and were very proud of their accomplishment. The students in other tiers were equally as focused, and all students asked to try tiered lessons again.

—Cynthia McKee (Teacher)

Calculating Density

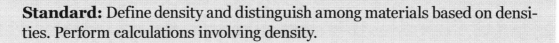

Subject: Chemistry
Grades: 10–12

Standard: Define density and distinguish among materials based on densities. Perform calculations involving density.

Key Concept: Properties of Materials

Essential Understanding: Students will know that different materials have different densities and will know how to determine the density of a material.

Background: The class has studied the definition of density and the formula for calculating density. Students have used practice problems to calculate density.

Tiered in Process

Tier I: Students will measure the volumes and masses of three different liquids. All samples can be measured in the same way. The students will calculate the density of each material and will determine the identity of the material from a chart of known densities.

Tier II: Students will measure the volumes and masses of three solids made of different materials. One solid will be a cube or rectangular prism, one will be a sphere or cylinder, and one will be an irregular shape. Each type of shape will require a different way to measure volume. The students will calculate the density of each material and will determine the identity of the material from a chart of known densities.

Tier III: Students will measure the volumes and masses of a solid, liquid, and gas. Each type of material will require a different method of measurement. A gas is also measured and calculated using different units. The students will calculate the density of each material and determine the identity of the material from a chart of known densities.

Assessment: Students will be given a performance task in which they are given an object and are asked to determine its density. Students will also be asked to describe how the arrangement of particles in a material relates to its density. (In other words, why do different materials have different densities?)

Created by Deborah Price

Real Teacher Comments

Density can be a difficult concept, and some students in basic chemistry still have trouble with the math needed for this calculation. Although students in all tiers are determining density, I have made each tier more challenging than the previous. I decided to assess students using a performance assessment rather than just checking their answers. I wanted to be sure that each student could determine density of an unknown and could also verbalize why different materials have different densities.

Designing a tiered lesson allowed me to provide activities that would challenge each group, rather than using one lesson pitched to the middle.

—Deborah Price (Teacher)

Calculating Average Speed

Subject: Science
Grade: 7

Standard: The Physical Setting

Key Concept: Speed

Essential Understanding: By comparing two different distances and times, one can calculate an average speed for two people or objects. Using this average speed, one can determine who was moving faster and how to manipulate the situation so they finish at the same time.

Background: The students have previously learned about how to calculate speed, distance, and time. They have done many examples where the time and distance are given to them, and they need to do their own calculations. They can also recognize the various units of measurement.

Tiered in Process

Tier I: Have two students individually run a set distance at least 10 times. Time how long it takes, and after recording the times, calculate each student's average speed. From this average speed for each student, create a graph that will show who was moving faster and explain how you determined your answer.

Tier II: Have two students individually run a set distance at least 10 times. Time how long it takes, and after recording the times, calculate each student's average speed. Then determine how much later the faster runner would have to start in order to reach the finish line at the same time as the other runner. Use a graph to make this determination.

Assessment: The teacher will observe the students as they are working on their experiment, checking for questions and misconceptions. After students have completed the experiment, the teacher will assess them on using the appropriate equation and numbers, as well as on their explanations and graphs.

Created by Allison Shakinis

Real Teacher Comments

I have found that students really enjoy doing experiments, but because all students do not have the same level of understanding, I often need more than one experiment that covers the same concept. I designed this tiered lesson to cover the essential calculations for speed. Students really enjoyed the opportunity to run down the halls and use stopwatches, so they didn't mind when they had to do math calculations and make graphs outside of their math class. They were having so much fun that students did not seem the least bit concerned that there were two different activities.

—Allison Shakinis (Teacher)

Allele Frequency

Subject: General Biology

Grade: 10

Standards:

○ Use analogies and models (mathematical and physical) to simplify and represent systems that are difficult to understand or directly experience due to their size, time scale, or complexity, and recognize the limitations of analogies and models.

○ Describe how, due to genetic variations, environmental forces, and reproductive pressures, organisms with beneficial traits are more likely to survive, reproduce, and pass on their genetic information.

Key Concept: Populations

Essential Understanding: Certain genetic combinations within a population can have an advantage in a certain environment, and therefore, those alleles will be passed on to offspring.

Background: Before beginning this lesson, students will know about genotype and phenotype for a trait. They will know that sickle-cell anemia is a recessive trait predominantly found in individuals of African descent. Prior to this lab, students will have used beetle models to calculate the allele frequency for specific populations. Using an exit card for assessment of that activity will help me determine tier placement for each student. Each group will be asked to calculate the allele frequency for a population over three generations, and then they will discuss why the allele frequency changed.

━━━ Tiered in Content ━━━

Tier I: These students still need practice determining genotype and phenotype frequency. Students working at this tier will use beetle models to determine genotype and phenotype frequencies under different environmental conditions.

Tier II: Students working at this tier will understand genotype and phenotype frequency and can mathematically determine the allele frequency for a population. They will model the effects of the sickle-cell allele through three generations of a small population living in a malaria-infected region and will then calculate the allele frequency for each generation. They will use the materials found at http://genetics-education-partnership.mbt.washington.edu/class/activities/HS/sickle-bean.htm.

Assessment: Teacher observation and student interviews during the activity may be used. A group discussion focusing on how and why the allele frequency changed may be conducted after the activity. A journal entry analyzing the results from the activity may also be used. Calculations will be checked for accuracy.

Created by Dawn Slein

Real Teacher Comments

My students were very motivated by this activity. They stayed focused on the tasks at hand for the entire period. The Tier I students all understood how to determine genotype and phenotype under various conditions by the end of the lab. The Tier II students were able to understand an abstract concept by moving from concrete to abstract in their lab. Both groups are ready to move on to the next topic, as evidenced by exit cards they completed after the lab and before they left for their next class.

—Dawn Slein (Teacher)

Energy Flow
in a Food Web

Subject: Science
Grade: 7

Standards

◆ Describe that all organisms, including the human species, are part of and depend on two main interconnected global food webs, the ocean food web and the land food web.

◆ Explain that energy can be transferred from one form to another in living things.

Key Concept: Energy

Essential Understanding: Energy is transferred from one organism to another. All living systems are connected and interdependent.

Background: A food web includes many food chains. Food chains always start with a producer that uses the sun's energy to make food. A food web is a complete and informative model of the complex feeding relationships in a community, rather than a single food chain. When an organism uses most of this energy for its life processes, only some of the energy is passed on to the next organism in the food web. A diagram called an energy pyramid shows the amount of energy that moves from one feeding level to another in the food web. At each level in the pyramid, there is less available energy than at the level below. The most energy is available at the producer level, and energy decreases as it passes through the consumers. Because of the amount of energy available, most food webs only have three or four feeding levels, with only a few organisms at the highest level in the food web. Students were placed in tiers based on their need for working with ideas and concepts on a continuum from simple to complex.

Tiered in Content

Tier I: Create a land food web using at least 12 specific organisms and four levels of organisms. Use the temperate deciduous forest or grasslands as the biome to create your web. Draw arrows to show the direction the energy flows. Label each organism with its name and whether it is a producer, consumer, or decomposer.

Tier II: Create a land food web using 20 organisms specific to on the Chaparral and four levels of organisms. Draw arrows to show the direction the energy flows. Label each organism with its name and whether it is a producer, consumer, or decomposer.

Tier III: Choose a biome and research what animals and plants live there. Create a land food web using at least 20 specific organisms found in the biome and show four levels of organisms. Draw arrows to show the direction the energy flows. Label each organism with its name and whether it is a producer, consumer, or decomposer.

Assessment: Rubrics will be used that include the following criteria: accuracy; whether four levels of organisms are included; whether the required number of organisms is present; whether drawings or pictures of organisms are present/colored; whether organisms are labeled with their names and whether they are producers, consumer, or decomposers; whether all arrows are drawn correctly showing energy flow; and WOW! (going above and beyond activity requirements).

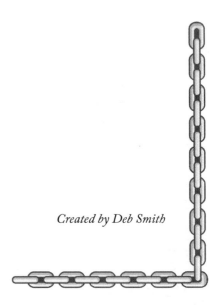

Created by Deb Smith

Real Teacher Comments

I developed this lesson for a unit on energy flow in living systems. In my seventh-grade class, my students run the gamut from struggling learners who have difficulty with grade-level material to high-ability learners who can move through material faster and handle abstraction. I like to provide all students with a way of demonstrating what they know by using tiered lessons. They are all focusing on the same learner outcomes, but they are showing their level of understanding in different ways.

In this lesson, those who need more direction, fewer choices, and scaffolding to be successful were placed in Tier I. Tier II students had less scaffolding, while Tier III students guided their own learning. Everyone used similar processes to produce similar products. When students shared their work, everyone was able to learn about biomes other than their own.

—Deb Smith (Teacher)

REFERENCES

Adams, C. M., & Pierce, R. L. (2006). *Differentiating instruction: A practical guide to tiering lessons in the elementary grades*. Waco, TX: Prufrock Press.

Coil, C. (2007). *Successful teaching in the differentiated classroom*. Marion, IL: Pieces of Learning.

Erickson, H. L. (2002). *Concept-based curriculum and instruction*. Thousand Oaks, CA: Corwin Press.

Gregory, G. H., & Chapman, C. (2002). *Differentiated instructional strategies: One size doesn't fit all*. Thousand Oaks, CA: Corwin Press.

Kingore, B. (2004). *Differentiation: Simplified, realistic, and effective*. Austin, TX: Professional Associates.

Passow, A. H. (1982). *Differentiated curricula for the gifted/talented: A point of view*. Ventura, CA: Ventura County Superintendent of Schools Office.

Tomlinson, C. A. (1999). *The differentiated classroom: Responding to the needs of all learners*. Alexandria, VA: ASCD.

Tomlinson, C. A. (2001). *How to differentiate instruction in mixed-ability classrooms* (2nd ed.). Alexandria, VA: ASCD.

Tomlinson, C. A. (2003). *Fulfilling the promise of the differentiated classroom*. Alexandria, VA: ASCD.

Ward, V. (1980). *Differential education for the gifted*. Ventura, CA: National/State Leadership Training Institute for the Gifted and Talented.

Winebrenner, S. A. (1992). *Teaching gifted kids in the regular classroom: Strategies and techniques every teacher can use to meet the academic needs of the gifted and talented*. Minneapolis, MN: Free Spirit.

ABOUT THE AUTHORS

Cheryll M. Adams is the director of the Center for Gifted Studies and Talent Development at Ball State University. She teaches graduate courses for the license in gifted education. For the past 30 years, she has served in the field of gifted education as a teacher of gifted students at all grade levels, director of Academic Life at the Indiana Academy for Science, Mathematics, and Humanities, and as the principal teacher in the Ball State Institute for the Gifted in Mathematics program. Additionally, she has been the founder and director of various other programs for gifted students. Dr. Adams has authored or coauthored numerous publications in professional journals, as well as several book chapters. She serves on the editorial review board for *Roeper Review*, *Gifted Child Quarterly*, *Journal for the Education of the Gifted*, and *The Teacher Educator*. She has served on the Board of Directors of the National Association for Gifted Children, has been president of the Indiana Association for the Gifted, and currently serves as president of The Association for the Gifted, Council for Exceptional Children. In 2002 she received the NAGC Early Leader Award.

Rebecca L. Pierce is associate professor of mathematical sciences at Ball State University and fellow at the Center for Gifted Studies and Talent Development. She teaches undergraduate and graduate courses in mathematics and statistics. For the last 35 years, Dr. Pierce has taught mathematics to elementary, middle school, high school, and college students. Dr. Pierce directs the Ball State Institute for the Gifted in Mathematics. Additionally, she worked as a Senior Research Engineer for Bell Helicopter and as a statistical consultant for a variety of industries. She has authored or coauthored numerous publications in professional journals, as well as several book chapters. She is the chair of Mathematics Day, a program for middle school girls interested in mathematics. She serves as a reviewer for *Roeper Review*, *Gifted Child Quarterly*, *Journal for the Education of the Gifted*, and *The Teacher*

Educator. She received the Leadership Award from the Indiana Association for the Gifted in 2002.

Dr. Adams and Dr. Pierce work with teachers throughout the United States and Europe toward establishing more effectively differentiated classrooms through the use of the CIRCLE MAP. In addition, they provide professional development and consultation in the areas of mathematics, science, identification, and program evaluation. They have coauthored and received three Javits grants from the federal government in partnership with the Indiana schools.